Working Would be Great if it Weren't for Managers

Thoughts on Business, Life, and Slackers

Gary W. Wells
MBA

Prologue

This book is a collection of my thoughts, ideas, and opinions taken from observing how co-workers and managers act in the work place. Unfortunately, much of what I have observed is negative. Many I have worked with have graduated from college, started their own families, entered the work force, moved up the corporate ladder, and proceeded to stomp on anyone that got in their way. I equate them to middle-school brats that got older but never really grew up. I hope someday we will get out of the "it's all about me" syndrome and begin to act like mature respectful adults.

Some of what you will read will be of a serious nature, and some not so serious. All of the stories have been massaged and intermixed. None are attributable to any one individual, manager, or co-worker. They are all my opinion on what happened and what shouldn't have happened. Some is pure fiction and other parts are opinion. My point is to tell my story and not indict anyone. If it is an indictment, it's on poor management, not individuals. Think of the stories as a composite of my career and life.

Some of you will be offended, others will not. If you're an abusive manager and not offended, perhaps you need some "emotional intelligence." Emotional intelligence is having a grasp of how others perceive you and how you treat your direct reports. Please take to heart my words. They will be a benefit to you. My sincerest hope and prayer is that you will be a better manager after contemplating my journey and suggestions.

I have found that corporate America has a severe learning disability. They have hired some of the best employees America has to offer, and then they absolutely refuse to utilize them to their fullest extent. It's the "not invented here syndrome" and don't bother me with the facts, my mind is made up. Therefore, they ignore and abuse some of the brightest employees around, and all of us suffer because of it.

Each company should be in the mode of developing their employees and then rewarding them for their hard work; the employee benefits, as well as the company. Both grow and become better and more competitive.

The more serious side of this book is designed to get corporate America to think about the type of people they hire into various positions, mainly supervisors, and how those supervisors should be managed and trained. Most are not managed properly, and most are never trained to manage people.

You will notice some contradictions throughout the book, actually acting with character and integrity vs. being a slacker. The two really don't mix. I wanted to create discussion and thought. Part will be to promote "slacking," just for fun, and the other will be to describe what I have observed. My hope is that you will be able to relate and say, yeah, I've been there.

You may ask what my background or expertise is in writing this book – I work in compliance. I have a B.S. and an MBA. I have been in this field for over twenty years. I drive/enforce the compliance process. I'm kind of like a Cop. People want a cop around when their house has been broken into, but not when you're giving them a ticket. I think I can safely say that in some groups I work with, I'm universally hated. It's a good field to be in, but it certainly has its ups and downs. You have to have a very strong constitution in my type of job. You have to stand your ground many times to make sure who you are representing is doing the right thing. In my field, you're to *Say what you do, do what you say, and prove it.* You must always be ready to defend your position on what you have done. I keep the makers of Zantac in business. That's Zantac for heartburn, not Xanax for anxiety and panic (I think I confused that once when on an interview. It didn't go over very well).

Chapter 1: Definitions and Descriptions

Let's start out with some definitions and descriptions. The best slacker around is one that is born into it. Perhaps due to genetics, or a good example, such as a slacker father, mother, or Grandfather, the slacker just naturally grows up and becomes a slacker. "Modeling" is definitely at work here. Modeling: the demonstration of a way of behaving to somebody, especially a child, in order for that behavior to be imitated. If this type of person were truly identified as a slacker, most, if not all, would deny their identity. This is truly sad. An individual that's a slacker should embrace their identity. They should work very hard at increasing their skills at becoming the best slacker they can be.

Anyone can be a slacker. You might be a part-time slacker or a full-time slacker. However, to be true to your heritage, you must have the mind of a slacker and be looking for opportunities to slack whenever you can.

A slacker is someone who looks for the opportunity to get out of work, relax, and generally take advantage of his employer. After all, your employer takes advantage of you, so why shouldn't the "advantage taking" be mutual?

The largest Slacker organization in the US is USA. What is USA; the United Slackers of America. USA's premise is based on the attitudes and beliefs of many different organizations. These organizations might be the American Federation of Laboring Slackers – Congress of Industrial Slackers, You Ain't Workin, American Federation of Slacking Teachers, National Slacker's Association, United Brotherhood of Slackers, "Special" Employees International Union, Associated Coalition of Real Narcissists, the U.S Congress, and Community Organizers.

Individuals and or groups that are involved in the USA are managers, co-workers, human resource representatives, and anyone who "works" hard or hardly works, at being a slacker.

USA is a collection of slackers throughout the United States that have a loose consortium on what slacking is. Nothing is well organized or written out, there are no meetings or newsletters. Just a general agreement on what it is to be a slacker. To have meetings, or newsletters, would require effort. This is not in the vocabulary of a slacker. Unless it's to take advantage of a situation in order to improve your position.

If possible, Slackers try to get their "personal" business done at work. That way, when they go home early for the evening, they are able to relax and slack at their leisure. See your time at home is your own to relax and have fun with your kids. Your time at work is to work, occasionally, because you still have bills to pay and kids to raise, but also to use it to your advantage whenever you can.

Within the next few pages, I will also give you examples on bad, pathetic management, and in addition, how to slack at work and home. Most of my examples will have to do with work. I have observed the most slacking there, and this is where I have best developed my own skills. Work is also where I have observed some of the worst management known to man. I think you will be able to relate. People are people no matter where they work and no matter what business they're in. It's just a shame so many managers abuse their position and abuse those that report to them. Most of them know they are bad, are too arrogant to admit it, or just don't care to do anything about it. Most recently, I have concluded that some are actually clueless about their behavior.

Chapter 2: Anatomy of Management Failure (The Indictment)

"All men can handle adversity, but if you really want to test a man's character, give him power." Abe Lincoln

Slacker Beezlebub –

My boss was not only my boss, but also one that did lower level work from time-to-time. Let's call him Slacker Bub for short. Bub came in with a resume and persona that was second-to-none. It was not until a few weeks later when his true identity showed through. Bub was performing some vibration testing on a product we were developing. We ran a hardware validation lab. Our vibration machine didn't have the ability to detect resonance conditions (the frequency at which a product or part will vibrate, like when your tire is not balanced properly and your car vibrates at 65 mph, but not at 70). Yet Bub stated that no resonance conditions were found. That was true; none were found because we didn't have the ability to detect any. When I approached him on this, he informed me that he had already sent out the report and that's the way it is, and that's the way it's going to stay. He said it was best not to amend the report, because of the "politics" involved, and how it might make our department look less competent in the eyes of others.

So, to a slacker, deception is a viable option; kind of like "situational ethics," whatever it takes to protect yourself, get your way, and your own point across. Winning is everything, and looking good even better.

Slacker Bub, throughout the next 7 years, played each of his manager's like a song. Some of the managers were very enamored with him, and the others that didn't know what enamored meant, just didn't have a clue.

By the way, we always wanted to buy Bub some industrial strength chap stick but we couldn't locate a lifetime supply. Severely chapped and puckered lips don't help in moving you up the corporate ladder.

Slacker Bub didn't like his day-to-day activities and decided his lifelong desire was to be in the limelight that meetings would provide. He decided to start teaching FMEA's (Failure Modes and Effect Analyses), took a 1-week seminar on the subject, and then promptly dubbed himself Mister FMEA. Soon he was relieved of additional duties, until he was doing nothing but FMEA's and attending meetings. Bub liked meetings; man did he like meetings.

Bub always reminded me of a little kid that would always run around trying to get attention. You've seen the kid. He's the one who walks with his chest out and his head held high, giving you the sense that he is here, he is better; he is Slacker Bub!

Bub was eventually promoted to a Director level. A foreign firm had purchased the company and had laid off many of the "producing" employees, yet Slacker Bub and various other workers remained. Many of the producing employees left the company. Slacker Bub was basically the last man standing in his area. He was bumped up a grade, received a 20% increase in pay, and became bonus eligible (this really follows the Peter Principle, being promoted to your level of incompetence). This meant he could receive as much as $15,000 in additional funds if he met his goals. One goal was to hire four additional grunt employees in order to build his empire. Oh, didn't I mention that in order to be a real manager, you must hire additional employees, even if you don't need them. This is to consolidate power, influence, and prestige, and wasting the corporation's money isn't a bad thing either.

Design Team –

Slacker Bub told me once that a co-worker, named Henry will always outshine you in this department and as long as you're in this department you will never get a promotion. That was so inspiring. Well, I did eventually get a promotion, Thanks be to God, and no thanks to Bub.

During one reorganization my company went through, Bub was doing all he could to damage my career. He was attempting to see where he could slot me where I would have less influence and impact. I couldn't let that happen, so I got smart. I slacked my way onto the department's "design team" (team for determining the background and education that the department employees would need to have in order to keep their jobs) and helped write my own job description, all with the expected experience and education. You could have put my picture beside the job description as one of the minimum qualifications. Bub was not a part of the "design team." I'm not sure what Bub had in mind, whether it was to play games or try to lay me off, I didn't know. I ended up getting that promotion, all to the dismay of Bub. He never congratulated me on my good fortune. I still reported to Bub, but he was not happy.

I've never really understood why managers go out of their way to harm the career of a subordinate or anyone else for that matter. It's just something that evades me.

Right before I left the firm, Bub called me to his office and wanted to give me a raise. He said I could have the raise only if I jumped through additional hoops. He wanted me to become a Certified Reliability Engineer. He stated his kids were too young for him to go back to school and devote any time to it and he didn't want to be away from them. My kids were 6 and 8 years old at the time, and Slacker Bub thought they were old enough for me to start school again. They didn't need me around. They were my kids, not his, thus the difference

While working for Bub, I had been supervising up to 12 temporary employees for the past 20 months, with all the responsibility and headaches that go with it. If you have ever managed temporary employees, you know it isn't a cakewalk, I'm sorry, a Slackwalk. Anyway, I had just finished my Master's in Business only four months before my meeting with Bub so you can understand that I was a little burnt out on school. During this time, I had more responsibility, more hours, and no extra pay. You're probably thinking stop your complaining this happens to everybody. Yeah you're right, I'm complaining. That's what slackers do best!

What was so interesting was the statement Bub made when he finally offered me a raise, he said, we would have given you more money but we didn't want to price you out of the market in case you wanted to leave and go somewhere else.

Not that I'm Peyton Manning, but imagine the Colts telling Peyton that they didn't want to price him out of the market in case he wanted to leave and go somewhere else. Oh, that's right; they went further than that and just simply let him go to the Broncos, unbelievable! If the employee, I mean slacker, is one that is delivering and doing a great job, price him out of the market so he will stay. That statement belongs in a

Dilbert comic. I gave him my resignation letter three weeks later. Even slackers have some pride.

On another occasion, Bub gave me the lowest increase I had ever received when working for the corporate world. After he told me the increase I would receive, he said, you probably think that's a slap in the face, but what else could I do? We were about to lose two co-workers, (due to their low pay) so we had to find the money somewhere. My motto from all of this is, "My sacrifice, their gain." Was this a slap in the face, can you say roto-rooter?

Slacker Comments –

Just like the show "Children Say the Darnest Things," so do managers. Managers and co-workers have a way at saying things that cut, hurt, or are just plain dumb.

As a slacker, you should never think about what you are going to say until after you say it. What does my brother-in-law say, "You should look before you leap." Slackers have a huge tendency to leap before they look.

Supervisors, in general, should really think about what they say, or at least how it will be perceived. Slacker Bub once made the comment, it shouldn't be too hard for you, you're the one with the Master's. He also said you're really using that Master's now and this really isn't that complicated, it's not brain surgery you know.

Look, if you are an intimidated, jealous fearful manager, and feel threatened by subordinates or co-workers, perhaps you should "jazz" up your resume so it looks like you have at least 15 years' worth of experience in the field you're working in, and have a Masters in something. That way, even though you know the truth, you won't be considered less qualified than those who report to you. The unwritten rule should be, never hire someone to work for you that has either had more work experience than you do, or more education. They just might make you look bad, especially if the higher ups don't have the same opinion of your work that you have.

Slacker Bub also stated once, You don't seem to understand the big picture and his boss, Slacker John stated, everyone should suffer some time or another in their career. I wanted to ask Slacker John, What do you call working for you? This wouldn't have been the slacker thing to do since that would have created many problems for me. A slacker will try very hard at not making waves.

One co-worker told me that life was like a totem pole. He was an engineer. Engineers think of themselves very highly. He said my head was found just under where his butt sits. Is that not a great statement or what?

Do you ever tease your co-workers? I do. It makes the work environment more enjoyable, and helps the day pass more quickly. As long as the teasing is done in fun, then everything should be okay, right? I was teasing a co-worker the other day, and told him that he needed to check out some power supplies for us to see if they worked properly. It was my responsibility and I knew this and so did he. He also knew I was teasing, and wasn't about to help me. Well, when Bub overheard me, he said, Gary, why don't you get off your lazy A#%, and do it yourself. What a motivator. What kind of thing is that to say to a subordinate? OUCH! Okay, if I'm truly a slacker, I should expect this.

One last thought for this section, if you're a manager, make sure you never apologize for anything. I have found that it must be some sort of unwritten rule for managers to squeeze, push, step, stomp, kick, ridicule, and bash employees, and never take responsibility for their actions. It's un-slacker like. It shows weakness. How else can you dominate your employees if you're apologizing for every little thing your say or do? You wouldn't be doing anything else.

MBO's –

I have found that MBO's (Management by Objectives) or really any type of individual goals can be quite counter-productive at generating success, but they work very well for your average slacking boss. Before you go off the deep end, let me explain.

The firm I worked for used these to achieve various goals. However, more often than not, and true to a typical slacker, Bub would set goals that he "felt" he could achieve, vs. what he should achieve. This was especially counterproductive, I mean helpful, when bonuses were linked to the MBOs.

Case in point, we were testing a product's ability to operate under certain environmental conditions. It was a health meter. I'm right handed, so when I tested the product, I always held it in my left hand. The product had an ambient temperature sensor located just above where you would inset the diagnostic probe. I would insert the probe with my right hand. My hand would never contact the sensor. However, the technician that worked for me was left-handed. She held the product in her right hand and inserted the probe with her left. Her right thumb rested right over where the sensor was located, just below the product's plastic case. This caused the product to give false temperature warnings to the user. We found this by mere accident, but determined that it was still significant enough to be reported in the test summary. Bub got irate and told me we had not specifically written the test plan to test that part of the product, so I was to remove the information from the test summary. Remember that slacker's think "twisting the truth" is just fine. Fortunately, a co-worker that was at Bub's level over heard my "discussion" about altering the test summary and convinced Bub that we should retest it. We retested, and proved that the sensor was indeed positioned in the wrong place. It was moved to a part of the product where it would continue to operate as intended and not give false readings.

Slacker Bub's bonus was linked to his MBO's and when the product would be launched. If not launched on the predetermined date, he could lose a substantial part of that bonus. On my next review, Bub informed me that I didn't understand the big picture, and gave me the lowest Cost of Living increase I had ever received in all the years I worked there. I really wanted to know if the big picture he was talking about was 25 inch, 35 inch, or a big 60-inch wide screen. I'm sure I would understand if it were the 60-inch screen. A new Phillips 72" HDTV flat screen plasma would have been nice too. Then again, perhaps if I had been bonus eligible like him, I would have had a better understanding of the big picture.

As a slacker, you should always think about your wallet. Follow the money trail and you'll see where the heart of the slacker truly lies.

Ruling by Intimidation –

Bub ruled by intimidation and fear. The atmosphere had been so totally corrupted by this man, that ingenuity, and a willingness to "go the extra mile" all but disappeared. He was arrogant, pompous, and ruled as if we were all in the military. You were to always recognize and know your rank and privilege, and that was lower than a slug.

The firm, meaning H.R., knew about the problems. The problems he created had been reported and complained about by many employees. Yet H.R., being H.R., always sided with the person they deemed had the highest rank. Slackers always do. It took almost five years before they intervened. Even then, it wasn't because he was a terrible manager, it was because he crossed an ethical line. Go figure. Bub was chastised and lost part of his bonus that year. The ethical issue was resolved, but he continued to be Bub.

If Bub had been managed properly from the beginning, the problems he exhibited would have come to light sooner and perhaps, just perhaps, he wouldn't have had to be punished for the ethical issue. H.R. never really dealt with the inter-personal/poor management issues Bub had with everyone. It was sad to see him flounder and even sadder that no one directly above him would do anything about it. If H.R. had stepped in to correct the problems and deal with them, he might have actually become a valuable productive manager.

Look, managing isn't easy. It sometimes requires us to step in and do the right thing no matter how painful. If you care for the employee, manager or not, and care for the company, H.R. and others need to do what they were hired to do, manage the company, including managers.

HR Slackers –

Let me give you a couple of examples of how H.R. can breed "Slackerism." It isn't really too hard, it's just a shame when it happens to good people. For example, the firm I worked for promoted one individual from the employee pool. Let's call her Slacker Kate. Kate had worked in various capacities for a number of years. Kate had a handle on the issues concerning the company and the perspective of all those involved. No one knew employees better than Kate. She offered the greatest hope for the employees of any H.R. rep. I had ever known.

Kate started out with promise and determination. She asked the right questions, listened, and even seemed to care. She would ask what your concerns were, what we were doing wrong and what were we doing right, all the right questions that should be asked. Yet in less than six months, she was given an "HR frontal lobotomy."

After her lobotomy, Kate developed an extraordinary attitude. She no longer had any concern with the issues. She exhibited pure "Slackerism." She gave you the impression that any time you called or came by with a question you were bothering her.

There was one occasion when I wanted to discuss some issues concerning Manager Bub dragging his feet on some promises he made. Don't ever believe the promises made by a slacker. Kate made the statement, stop your whining and complaining. Well I was whining and complaining. What's a slacker to do? If you're not entitled simply because you're you, then what's the use in slacking at all! However, really, if you're a manager and you make promises, they should be kept or you should have enough integrity and character to explain why.

Did you know slackers have a theme song? Perhaps you've heard it. Remember the song by The Miracles, "I'm just a, just a Love Machine, and I won't work for nobody but you?" Well, replace the lyrics with, I'm just a, just a slackin machine and I won't slack for nobody but chew! Nevertheless, I digress.

Kate started sitting on every employee team available. She really didn't contribute much of anything, and as a slacker, how could she. She needed to be doing something to justify her paycheck.

We had one employee team that struggled against great odds, and pushed forth many new programs that would greatly help the company and employees in general. So when it came time to thank them, only Kate and the employee leader of the group were rewarded financially. Not a large sum, I think it was around $250-$500 dollars, but still a slap in the face to the other employees who had worked on the team. I guess the company wanted to encourage employees to step up and take on leadership roles. Kate was already in a leadership role, so I'm not sure why she would have been rewarded.

It seems, or at least in my experience, H.R. departments are unreceptive to the various issues that confront employees. I do hope they do a better job where you work. I have learned throughout the years to fight the battles worth fighting, and the others, attempt to let them slide. That's not easy. Life is just too short sometimes.

Reviews and the Budgeting Process –

During slow work times, I always tried to either attend in-house courses or be involved with employee teams. Slackers love employee teams.

One team was designed to discuss reviews and the budgeting process, and make recommendations on their findings. Our reviews were always top down and sometimes, very much "in your face." Read it, sign it, get out of my office; get out!

What's a review for, if not to review performance and enhance the employee's ability to serve himself all while providing very little to the corporation? A good number of reviews are a popularity contest. If you're a good slacker, and can "massage" your boss just right, you're given glowing comments on how great you are. If you're not a slacker, it can be all business, and sometimes the comments are complete fabrications. Local management and H.R. departments never have problems with fabrications. If it doesn't hurt them, who cares? Don't ever get H.R. involved in a dispute with your boss; you won't win. It's not their job to seek the truth; remember its H.R.'s job to side with the person with the highest rank. Slackers are very loyal to power, influence, and position. That's why so many of them worked in this H.R. Department.

I had one review where 97% of it was completely distorted. That's a nice way of saying distorted. Distortion, Deficiency, and Contamination (DDC) do not belong in any review. Distortion is defined as, making something larger or smaller than it really is, Deficiency, leaving important things out, and Contamination, adding things that are not relevant or true. Yet slackers love DDC.

An employee team that I was on was discussing how reviews could be fairer and more performance related. We were trying to implement what is known as a 360-degree review process. This is where you review your supervisor, he reviews you, and a hand-full of your "internal customers" co-workers participates as well. You are allowed to see all of the comments that have been given to your boss and passed on to you anonymously. It prevents a bad boss from fudging on a review, while it gives a good boss a better understanding of your performance throughout the past year. Of course, employees need to be trained on what belongs in a review and what doesn't. That would take time and money. Doing what's right always requires effort, and most Slackers will follow the "Way of the Slacker," exerting the least amount of effort in every situation.

The team discovered that our budgeting process occurred during the fall, while the reviews didn't happen until the spring of the following year. We discovered that the supervisors would assign merit pay, and any COL adjustment during the fall, and when they would do the review, they would "slot" the ranking to match what they had decided earlier. This is excellent strategy. To find a way at controlling the budgeting process and lessen the effects of the 360-degree review was just superb.

When we brought this "problem" up to an H.R. rep., Slacker Kate, she stated what we slackers always say, that's the way we have always done it why do we need to change? We will just inform the supervisors of the timing problem and everything will be okay. What's that about beachfront property in Arizona?

Do you go to the bathroom, eat your dinner, and then wash your hands after? Is that the way it's done in your home? That isn't how it's done in mine. Perhaps you would prefer your surgeon to wash his hands after the procedure. What H.R. wanted was to continue to keep the cart before the horse, it shouldn't have worked that way, but it did.

Slacker supervisor Bub found a way around providing the comments of the 360 to the employee. He stated that he would gather the comments, and in order to protect the identity of those participating in the review, he would massage the information and put it in his own words. I then noticed something. After this new 360-process had started, Bub apparently had been talking with my co-workers about what he wanted in my review. Suddenly things known only to Bub and myself appeared on my review, but they were supposed to be comments from my internal customers. Since I wasn't allowed to review the comments as is, (massaged remember) I couldn't ascertain whether it was the truth or not.

Managers do have a way at manipulating the truth to suit their purposes. Touché Bub! Touché!

ARR –

ARR – (Annual Review Retaliation), this is where you may have reviewed your boss the year before and not have given him a very good rating. This really ticks them off, especially when their boss makes them address the various findings as cited by you and other direct reports. What an unethical boss then does is this, if they have an issue with your performance, real or false, they wait to address this until your next annual review. That way they can impact your raise, bonus, or both, maybe even your career. You see, they are really upset with your view of their performance last year and did not have an opportunity to retaliate until now. If they really had an issue with your performance, they should have said something long before review time. That is what a good boss would do. But that would not have accomplished what they actually wanted, punishing you for giving them a bad review the year before. When this happens, there isn't a lot that you can do about it. The information is often fabricated, unsubstantiated, and biased. Your left shaking your head and looking around trying to determine where this all came from.

Dead Weight Employees –

Bub, at one point in his career, was acting as an Innovation Champion whatever that meant. He could never really tell you nor could the firm. I think he was supposed to inspire us to bigger and better things. He would attend department meetings, project meetings, and generally try to bring about employee innovation. This new role was never really defined, (superb for a slacker), so he didn't inspire much of anything. He did try, but seemed to be more of a bother than anything else.

I remember he would also be the chairperson for our project "Post Mortems." The post mortems were designed to clarify the issues concerning the product we had just launched. It certainly had merit; it just wasn't implemented very well. We used the "Colorful Hats" method. It's was a mechanism for breaking down your opinions into different forms. The Red hat was your emotional side. The Black hat was for your logical analytical side, etc. This was all slacker and dandy, except for the fact we paid big bucks to send people to be trained in the Colorful Hats method. We could have gotten just as much out of it by just stating what we observed, thought, and what we believed went right and wrong and how we could improve for the future.

Most anything you do is really common sense. You don't have to make it harder than it is; except of course if you're a slacker. The slacker will make it seem as hard as possible, thus making it hard for others to understand. This puts the slacker, at least in his own mind, as being above others, and as more important, more intelligent. Kind of, like when you were a kid, and would shout, "I know something you don't know!" I think most employees just thought the Post Mortems were a waste of time, simply because we never learned from them to improve the next time around.

After Slacker Bub was in this position for, I think, 2 years, the company asked, what are we getting out of this guy? What did they do, they gave him another role of being a Project Leader Champion. Slacker Bub would champion the project leaders. Did they need championing? Did they need a leader? Did they need help? Sure, most Project Leaders needed help, but not from a Project Leader Champion. Slackers really do want to help, especially if it keeps them from doing real work.

We had, in our development process of new equipment and processes, what we called Project Leaders. They handled most of the planning and staffing needs for the development team. Most project leaders were pulled from one political battle to another. All had to compromise from time to time. Generally, the compromise had an effect on product features, and occasionally quality, but whatever the compromise, it wasn't to affect the timeline or their bonus.

The timeline was and is the "god" of project development. I will not debate the significance of the timeline. I will debate politics and the timeline when it affects quality.

As stated, politics often affects budget, quality, and time to market. It always does. The politics of the matter and our inability to have the quality we needed destroyed my company's engineering department, or was it our slacker mentality?

Supervisor Bub once told me, I better learn how to play the corporate game (politics) or I would never move up the corporate ladder. He was right. After a point, I did stop moving up the corporate ladder; after all, I was a slacker. I responded with, it isn't about moving up the corporate ladder, it's about doing your job to the best of your ability and hopefully helping your company make some money along the way. It's about integrity and as the Bible says "And whatsoever ye do, do it heartily as to the Lord, and not unto men." Colossians 3:23. I digress once again. This really isn't how a slacker thinks, is it?

Shortly thereafter, our engineering group was decimated due to a buyout. I had left some four months earlier, and Bub left about a year after I did. Well, so much for playing corporate politics Bub.

Right before we were to become ISO certified, (International Standards Organization - a European quality kind of thing) there was a frenzy to get our house in order. Things we had always done, and some of it well, now had to be documented. This was good. It forced us to take a look at our methods and determine if they were working, and if not, improve them.

But being ISO certified doesn't ensure product quality, or that you are doing things right, it only ensures that you document what you do, and do it that way, even if it's wrong. That's the ISO way.

The fun part about this is that we had to come up with a division mission statement. The day before the ISO inspectors arrived, a mission statement bounded up on our cube-step. We were all supposed to place it in a prominent area of our office for all to see.

Mission statements are to be a group effort. You want buy-in from all, if possible. I know not all employees will go along with different thoughts and ideas, but that's life.

We were to live, breathe, and sleep the mission statement. I kept Bub happy by memorizing the mission statement and verbalized it in a robotic tone. Not to him, but to other slackers I worked with. Try this yourself (robotic tone) we are committed to exceeding our customer's expectations though excellence and continuous slacking in all that we do. Well "slacking" wasn't really the word we used.

This statement came in handy in my Master's program. When we wanted to slack, instead of coming up with a group mission statement in one of the classes I was in, we just adopted this one. Remember to be a true slacker; plagiarism is the sincerest form of flattery.

Mission Statements are important, but they are only so important. If you consider the "big picture" for a moment, they are often written by higher-level managers, adopted by the employee community as a whole, and then never heard of again. They have very little meaning at the worker-bee level.

I remember going to an internal interview to check out a Project Management Consultant position. The first question out of the manager's mouth, let's call her Slacker Dim Wit, was can you recite our company's mission statement? Oh please! What does this really have to do with whether I will be able to do a good job or not. You should want to know about my qualifications, experience, and education. How I will handle stress and ambiguity, and how I will work with my new co-workers, not whether I know the mission statement. Maybe you should learn something of importance like the Declaration of Independence, Bill of Rights, or maybe the U.S. Constitution, something of real lasting value. Well, I recited the division statement to her, not the company's statement, and no, I didn't recite it in a robotic tone.

I never got that job, thank goodness; it ended up being nothing more than a glorified, high level, administrative assistant position. Now I know there isn't anything wrong with being an administrative assistant. If I had been a good slacker, I would have spent more time on memorizing the company's mission statement rather than concentrating on what was important.

I went back to my office, and shared with Slacker Bub (that was a mistake) on what went down at the interview. Bub let me know that he once got a job simply because he knew the company's mission statement. This is the same guy that once told me that he felt he talked more intelligently on the phone when he wore a tie. Wow! Go figure. Of course, Bub also lived in a prominent nearby community because of the address. He felt it would make him more acceptable to the powers to be if they knew where he lived. Maybe it did.

Entrance Exam –

Many fortune 500 companies these days use entrance exams/pre-tests to determine if you meet their minimum "qualifications." They may also be used to determine if you even get an interview. These types of tests are designed to have only one correct answer out of many that may be partially correct, but supposedly, only one is actually correct. Problem is, depending on the company, your experience and education, any one of the answers may be the correct one. It all depends. Just because you had an outside organization develop the questions and answers, does not mean that their build and interpretation of the test makes it right. Sure, it's right in their mind, because they built the test, but depending on your circumstances, where you work, the type of business you are in and who you report to, there are many factors that drive the "right" answer. Now if they really want to determine your "worth" then how about making the test straight forward with only one correct answer. No, they want to play "head games" and see if you can select the answer(s) that they think should be the correct one. Since there is no true right and wrong answer, it's really just an opinion. You can disagree if you like but you should be concerned with determining reasoning capabilities, or in the ability of the candidate to do the job? Shouldn't experience, background, and education matter? If not, there is no reason to ask for a resume, do a background check, or even check references. Just simply have applicants take your entry exam, and if they choose the opinion answers you like, then hire them.

There's more to an employee, much more than what a simple psychological opinion exam will show. I have never liked a stacked deck against me or anyone else. Take ice skating or gymnastics in the Olympics; the scoring is all based on opinion. I will take a game with a score over opinion every time. If you and I are playing one-on-one in Basketball, and the clock runs out with me ahead, I win. It's plain and simple, no opinion. Maybe you looked better than I did while playing, but the score says it all. Tim Tebow and the Denver Broncos didn't look good for many of the games they played in 2011/2012, but at the end of the game, the score made all of the difference, and making the playoffs didn't hurt either.

So cling to your entry exams, it does make the interviewing process easier, but the interview and the candidate's experience should carry more weight, much more weight than the exam. I think the entry exam allows those interviewing to be lazy and not rely on good old fashioned methods for determining if a candidate will be a good fit or not. You need to stop being lazy and do what's right. Are you capable of that?

What? -

I once interviewed with a company out of central Florida. The interview started out like so many others. They have you first talk to HR. They walk you through the company benefits, 401k, vacation, etc. They then had me do a group interview with five possible co-workers and/or direct reports. You do not want direct reports doing an interview of their possible boss. It's not a good thing. Sometimes they have applied for the very position that you are interviewing for and are irritated and resentful that you are interviewing for it and they are not. Never the less, companies continue to do this as a practice.

Just some background before I continue. The position was at a Director level. I would be working in compliance with ~ five direct reports. You would need to have a solid background in compliance, good interpersonal skills, and supervisory experience.

The interview with the five continued. They asked questions about my background, education, and how I would handle various circumstances. For the most part, they were very cordial and easy on me, except for one individual. Maybe they wanted him to act a certain way or not, I don't know. He sat directly opposite of me and just stared at me the entire time. When he did speak, he was as obstinate as he could be. I answered him in a very reasonable manner and decided to ignore the less than professional behavior. Once again, maybe the plan was for him to act like a jerk, I don't know. Maybe they wanted to play a game and see how I would react. Is this really, how a professional organization should behave? This has happened in other interviews as well. I believe it's a strategy. Someone plays good cop while another plays bad. Either way, I believe I recognized it for what it was childish behavior.

They then passed me on to the hiring manager and one of her significant others. This part of the interview went well. I noticed something along the way though, not one question had to do with how I would manage direct reports, not one. All had to do with the technical side. I'm pretty good on the technical side. The problems I have noted throughout my career have to do with poor management and in not managing direct reports as well as we should; not treating them as human beings, and not treating them with dignity and respect. The interview continued and I felt like I was doing well. They finally decided to wrap it up. The hiring manager asked one last question. Do you ever get nervous? Let me explain further. When she asked this, she and the other interviewer acted as if they were upset with me because I was showing so much confidence and poise. They were actually upset that I had done so well. So I responded to the question, do you ever get nervous, with, sure I do, that's what Zantac (heartburn medicine) is for. In fact, I had taken a Zantac before I started the interview and kept a bottle of water with me the entire time to keep from getting "dry mouth." They laughed nervously at my response. They wanted to know how I handle stressful situations. I proceeded to tell them that you envision a number of different scenarios by looking at the worst case, best case, and most likely case. You also approach those that have the most information about what you are trying to accomplish to get their input. This method, combined with good planning, usually does the trick. If not, you go back to the drawing board and determine what your next steps should be. A little praying doesn't hurt either.

Well, needless to say, they apparently didn't like my response and that I did so well at presenting myself during the interview. I was not offered the position. Based on what I saw, and their approach to the interview, I'm not sure that was a bad thing. I don't like being rejected by anyone, but God knows better than I do. When you're on the outside looking in, it's very hard to determine if it will be a good fit or not. When you get this type of feedback, it's a good signal that something isn't right and that you should probably move on. Not concentrating on my ability to manage direct reports was a Red flag that they had some major problems.

Strategic Business Development –

We had a Strategic Business Development (SBD) department where I worked. They were supposed to analyze internal business needs and determine new markets and products to meet those needs.

I have to say that those who worked in SBD were some of the most arrogant people I have ever met. Many of them had come from the ranks of sales and marketing, or so I was told. The head of SBD was Slacker Kevin. You entered his office through double-doors embossed with Gold and Silver. You walked down a long dark hallway, and on either side of the hallway were pictures of Kevin working and directing in many different capacities. The pictures were of him and his many different travels, Paris, Budapest, Moscow, Beijing, Venezuela, New York, Chicago, Cuba, Waco, etc.

Kevin had the office with all the trimmings. He had a big desk; I mean huge, an overstuffed chair, large expensive pictures and wall hangings, and a humongous slacker table for which to hold meetings.

Kevin worked in the administration building, with quite a few of the other arrogant managers. I often said that if the lights went out in Admin, as we called it, that it would glow for hours from the amount of arrogance that was found there. They wouldn't have to restore power for days, maybe months.

I had once applied for a position to work in SBD but never got an interview or heard any word on who they hired. I called Kevin and asked if I could meet with him to find out more about his area and what it would take to work there. Kevin invited me in, sat me down in a really small chair in front of his desk, and asked what I needed to know. Looking up at him seated on his throne, I reminded him about the position in which I was interested. Kevin said he remembered my job bid. Talking in a condescending manner, he told me that before I could work in his area, I would need to work in marketing, then sales, and then in marketing once again before they would even consider someone like me, how dare me. A "subject" like me should not have even approached his Excellency.

A pattern had started to form here. I had been on many internal interviews and began to think that those interviewing me didn't have a whole lot to keep them busy. It seemed as if they would schedule interviews as a way to keep them busy and give them some entertainment throughout the day. I do believe that some of the people I talked with had never even considered me for the position; they just wanted to see me squirm for a while. Some questions they asked were valid, and some didn't make any sense at all, like the mission statement question. Have you ever seen a slacker squirm, it's not a pretty sight.

Let me tell you a story of how effective our SBD group was at identifying new cutting edge products and businesses. At one time we held 80% of our market. If you know anything about market share that's huge and it constitutes millions. A small start-up firm had approached us with a new convenient technology that would revolutionize the industry. SBD, along with a consulting firm, decided that our customers wouldn't want it. We had 80% of the market, so who cares, get lost; don't bother us again. The start-up firm was purchased by a competitor, who promptly infused them with the seed-money they needed to complete development. Within ten years, our market share dropped from 80% to 34%, with an untold loss of millions. SBD (remember, marketing, to sales, and back to marketing again) had blown it. Not only were we playing catch up, the product we developed to compete with it had numerous quality problems (certainly no problems that would constitute harm to a customer) but problems that cost additional thousands to fix.

SBD, in their all-glowing arrogance, took no blame, as a slacker should never, ever assume blame, and continued in their arrogant ways.

As an interesting side bar to all of this, let me tell you a little about the development process of the product we created to compete against our new threat.

It was deemed the "Dawn" project. For a new Dawn was upon us. The firm stated that there would be a select number of employees that would work on the project. They also stated that only the best the firm had to offer would be assigned to the project. I did work on the project from time to time, but think about that statement for a moment. If you're a slacker you can think about this at work (ponder it) and if you're good, think about it for an hour or so, I'll wait....................., done, good, back to our story. This type of attitude immediately separated the employees into the "have" and "have-nots." On the political level, it's called "class warfare." If you weren't on the project, what did that make you? Well, it makes you a "slacker has been."

For those on the team, they had motivational lunches in the company courtyard with hamburgers, hot-dogs, cake and ice cream. They gave away gifts, such as, Dawn soap-on-a-rope, Dawn pen and pencil sets, Dawn tire gauges, Dawn hats, Dawn jackets, Dawn shirts, Dawn you name it. This was great if you were on the team, but what if you were not. Unfortunately, a number of those on the team were there out of favoritism, not necessarily because they were the most qualified. Being a favorite is very important to a slacker. You can do more through favoritism than you can from being qualified.

The management team that was running the project was given the mandate to develop the project and get it launched as quickly as possible. Remember; we were losing a ton of sales to our wiser competitor. Not only did we develop it in record time; we cut corners, and ignored valid data and information along the way. Once launched, the quality problems showed up out in the field and bit us like a Pit Bull. Due to SBD's arrogance, and the internal politics in developing the product, we ended up having a voluntary recall. It was the largest recall in our company's history to that point. A losing track record like this sticks longer and better than your slacker cousin-in-law sacked out in your back bedroom.

A firm had recently purchased us. They took a good long look at our department and decided that it wasn't up to par, so they annihilated Engineering after the buyout. They didn't blame SBD for the loss of market share or in not obtaining the new technology when they had the chance, they blamed Engineering.

Slacker (SBD) Kevin eventually left the company. Perhaps it was to follow his advice, marketing, sales, and then back to marketing, I don't know.

Finance Logic? –

A position opened up in our Finance department. I was only months away at obtaining my MBA, so I thought it would be good to obtain a position in an area that related to my degree. Plus it would be good to get away from Bub.

The slacker in charge of Finance was Slacker Tom. Tom reviewed my job bid and decided he didn't have enough time to spend with me in order to bring me up to speed. He did have the time to hire a foreign exchange worker from Europe that would only be with us for one year. That way he could go through the entire hiring and training process again in a year. Hey, if it makes sense to Tom, it should make sense to you and me.

I must admit, the woman he hired was a lot better looking than me. She certainly had better looking legs. I believe she was from the "Swedish Ski Team" from a few years back. I could have worn my hair differently, started wearing makeup, shaved my legs, but if you've seen me, that really wouldn't have helped.

Power Play –

Bub and I ran an internal hardware test lab for a while. There was one episode where I was supposed to test a new product by checking its ability to survive 6 drops, once on each side, from a height of 40 inches. This was a critical test for us since our product was hand-held and easily dropped.

We talked about timelines earlier and I want to explain how slacker project leaders can use this to their advantage. Slacker project leader Mo knew that dropping our new product and it possibly failing our specs, could cause us to slip schedule and thus interfere substantially with his bonus, so he played the "Stall game." Wait until the last minute to test, and if it fails, you can't do anything about it because it's too late. Just accept it as a "project risk" and move on.

I requested samples in advance long before the critical milestone was to occur to authorize us to turn on production. Mo wouldn't deliver. I eventually performed an end run and went directly to the Engineering production manager in charge. I told him I was in need of three samples. He graciously provided them to me.

The product top and bottom case had only a press fit. No screws were utilized to hold them together. The product performed very well, much better than our other products. It did fail on the last drop. The product case opened slightly. Any opening at all was a failure. This made Mo very angry. He was upset that I had circumvented his authority and obtained the samples on my own. This interfered greatly with his "stall plan." He informed me I was to never do this again. We were too close to turning on production and didn't need any problems right now. He accused me of being a "malcontent." If you can't beat em, or intellectually spar with them, then call them names. That always helps.

All thanks go to the design engineers working on the project. They had made provisions for screws to be attached, one at each corner of the product, thus saving us valuable time in rework. I re-tested the product and it performed flawlessly.

My point is this. Slacker Mo had no intention of adding screws to keep the product intact. I understand that it added cost through additional labor and parts, but the fact was it was failing a specification that he had previously agreed upon. His bonus was in jeopardy. What does Rush Limbaugh say? Follow the money trail! Follow the money trail!

Of all the fads my firm latched onto, one of the most curious was Broad-Banding. Broad-Banding was a form of pure socialism. Stalin and Lenin would have definitely approved. Were they slackers?

It was designed to make everyone the same. For instance, all engineers were thrown into the same pool. The pay range, at the time, was from 25,000 to 75,000 per year. There were no more career levels and no way to gauge where you were and where you wanted to be. There were things written down that supposedly told you how to develop your career, but there was no ladder, and no carrot. The language was so nebulous that you had no idea how to move up.

I was a "Zebra" for a while and later became a "Lion." I always thought those that came up with this system should have a level entitled "Baboon," but instead, I think they were dubbed "Elephants." We needed a W.T. Grants close by so we could buy our "Garananimals" outfits to match our "level" orange shirt on white pants, or white shirt on orange pants

To move from one band to another required an increase in responsibility of 50% or more. This was never spelled out. Fifty percent to one manager might be 70% to one or 35% to another. No one knew and H.R. wasn't saying. Slackers love this kind of language. That way they can never be nailed down on anything.

This was all designed to slow down or eliminate promotions. Rather like calling a COL allowance merit pay. Merit pay is beyond the call of duty. COL is linked to inflation. The best among us might get a 3.5 % increase while the worst would get a 3% increase. It was just too much of a pain for managers to ever give someone less than 3%, because that would imply they hadn't met our firm's basic performance requirements, and that would then require the employee to be put on a "work plan" so they gave everyone the same amount.

I finally did get one H.R. rep. to admit the difference between COL and merit pay, but she still refused to admit it publicly.

Weekly Time Cards –

I know you have read about these in Dilbert comics, and in case you thought they were all a figment of Scott Adams imagination, think again. The department I worked in had an obligation/desire to count everything as development. That way they could claim it as a tax deduction. The sad thing is, it required all workers to "pad" their time. For instance, if you had worked more than 20 hours in a week as administrative time, you were required to spread it over all the projects you were working on, whether you worked on them or not. I had more than once, during slow work periods, reported 20 hours or more on my time card as administrative time, because that's what it was. Slacker Bub called me in his office and let me know that I was never to do this again. Whether this was initiated by him or his boss, I don't know. Either way, I was instructed to "pad." From then on out, I would spread my time over each project on which I was working. My superiors were delighted. I never heard another complaint.

This practice is very common in the industry, especially among consultants and contract houses. Anyway, no matter whether it was the truth or not, you were never allowed to claim administrative time. All of your time had to be allocated to a project even if it were false and blew the budget.

Case in point, we were working for a firm in the South. We were late in finishing the build and the validation of the structure and the equipment found inside. So, what did we do to rein in the time-line? Originally there was maybe a hand full of individuals assigned to the validation effort. So, to make things "go more quickly," we assigned up to nine additional individuals to the effort and had top level managers fly down to ensure that we were doing our job. It didn't matter that not all the equipment was installed and ready to test. And since this was our current situation, the validation effort couldn't take place, thus the time-line could not be reigned in. You were to pretend you were working. Unfortunately being productive is not always the goal. So, 5 managers were flown down to be on-site, with some having a bill rate of a least $150 per hour to manage nine employees. You do the math, say 100 per hour for the employees, (9 x 100 = $900) and say an average rate for the managers of $130 (5 x 130 = $650), times at least 8 hours per day at a minimum of 5 days per week. What is that? $62,000 per week! Our entire budget for validation was only $650,000. Wow? Wow! What more can I say. A fool and his money is soon departed. We blew the budget and blew it rapidly.

One manager, Curly, sat behind his laptop for more than 40 hours per week and "managed" a project time-line that was prebuilt for him. All he needed to do was update it each day or every other day. That never took more than an hour and I am being generous in saying an hour. He even worked weekends managing the time-line. He never spent one minute doing work that would have been valuable. Valuable would mean work at validating the equipment and getting us out under budget and within the time given. The point was to get in, build, validate, and get out as quickly as possible. This would allow us to make money and move on to the next job.

Shortly there-after they laid me off and gave me one day's severance. Wow, why even bother with the paper-work? The office closed within a few weeks later. What's the Bible say "vengence is mine sayeth the Lord, I will repay, I will repay" and God did. I still don't know why they even bothered giving me any severance.

Skills Data Base –

During one of our reorganizations, all of us slackers were required to develop a "Skills Data Base" and turn it in to our immediate supervisor. What they never told us was what it was for, or how detailed it needed to be. Being scared about how the information would be used, and being slackers, we developed the database on company's time and made it as detailed as possible. If you knew how to use a Digital Multi-meter, write it down. If you knew how to navigate Windows, write it down. If you knew how to change the toilet paper in the bathroom, write it down. I think you get the picture. What we were afraid of, and for good reason, was that they would use the list to determine if we were qualified to do our jobs and compare us to our co-workers. Well, that's exactly what they did. For example, one employee, who had a degree in Chemistry, was "Mapped" and placed in our software validation department. She had absolutely no experience or training in software validation, but what should that matter? She floundered in our department and could offer nothing of value. She eventually reapplied for her previous position six months later. That's the earliest she would be allowed to switch positions. She got her old job back and left shortly thereafter.

What's Mapping? It was a means, based on your skills, to slot you in a position where you were supposed to be the most qualified. Well, qualifications had nothing to do with it. They put you where they wanted to, all based on a whim. I had to compete with six other employees for my job. I was ultimately chosen as the best one for my position, go figure.

Slackers should always try to promote each other into more lucrative positions. You should try to do this within the company you work for, or better yet, let your protégé' tag along with you from company to company and when you move up the ladder, so does he.

I remember one manager who did this very thing. H.R. was never very good at holding managers accountable. So, whenever a position was approved, it had to be posted internally first, even if the manager had someone else already in mind. The manager would do his very best to dance and side step through the process. They would even schedule interviews with prospective employees, knowing very well that they didn't have a chance-in-a-million at the job.

Where I worked, I always considered the job bid process kind of like a lottery. Sometime or another you just might hit the right numbers, most of the time you were just rolling the dice and coming up blank.

One manager looked at my resume and job bid, and knew it was a perfect match. Except this time, he was so determined in his decision (don't confuse me with the facts, my mind's made up) he interviewed only two people, I was not one of them. One of those individuals, he eventually hired. He interviewed one other, only because he was forced to give him a shot. The employee he hired didn't even meet the minimum qualifications for the position and H.R. didn't care, as long as the manager was happy, everyone was happy.

Take Bub for instance. Bub did his very best to hurt and belittle people his entire career. The things he would do and the things he would say were very hurtful, yet he was never really held accountable.

Listen to me very carefully slackers, even if we have a loose agreement and consortium on what we are, we must never choose to deliberately hurt other slackers.

Slackers hurt emotionally, physical, mentally, and even spiritually. The rest of the world doesn't understand us, and if we don't support each other, then no one will.

Latest Trends –

Does the company you work for latch on to every trend that comes their way? If you think about it for a moment, most of what the latest guru is saying is all about common sense, and nothing more. Yet, practically all of the managers I used to work for would give you the impression that what they were hearing and reading was some kind of new revelation. They would never ask if it had worked anywhere else. They would never ask if it would actually work for us. They would go to great lengths to do market research for a new product, but never do any on this new method for "leap-frogging" us ahead of our competition. If you think about it, if our competition were also doing it, wouldn't we all just end up playing par?

We practiced TQM, SPC (which is very good by the way), ISO, and "Best in the Business." We would read "Slackplace 2000," "Slackers Redeemed," "The Art and Practice of the Slacker Organization," "Working Would be Great if it Weren't for Managers" an excellent read by the way, and last but not least, "The Seven Habits of Highly Effective Slackers."

The Seven Habits we adopted were:
1) Come in late and leave early.
2) Always take extra time at lunch.
3) Pad your time card.
4) Smooze your boss.
5) Pawn work off on others.
6) Never make another slacker look bad.
(Remember the loose consortium we have) and
7) Blend, Blend, and Blend.

If you're a manager and you have a subordinate bring you a business plan that could possibly make the company some extra money, determine if you can claim it as your own, and if not kill it.

I had recently written a business plan for my company that would have generated almost $90,000 in additional revenue per year. And over ten years that would be how much, $900,000.

I wanted to open our test lab to outside clients. Quite often, during non-development cycles, our lab would be idle. Why not generate some revenue while we were idle? I wrote the plan, presented it to my boss Slacker Bub and never heard another thing about it. Right before I left the company, I submitted it to Bub's boss and ultimately his boss. Guess what, no comments, nothing. They were rolling in so much dough, that $900,000 was apparently of no value.

Some companies would jump at the chance to make additional money and keep slackers busy, but most have a tendency to miss out on what's important. If it's not our idea (invented here) we don't want to hear it.

All of us want to be productive and one of the worst things you can do, even to a slacker, is not keep them busy doing something.

Bub has got to be the greatest slacker I have ever known. He has got to be the epitome of what the ultimate slacker is or ever wants to be. I could write an entire chapter on Bub, and I will.

If you are still with me, I commend you. You are very patient, or just don't have anything better to do. I do hope you're reading this at work though. Right before lunch or right after.

Anyway, Bub had everything every slacker wants, power, influence, and the freedom to abuse his position and his employees. He had very little education for the position he held, yet he moved up the corporate ladder with ease. He did this by following his boss from job to job. He was promoted each time his boss was. It was great. He was protected and nurtured by his boss, and was never held accountable for much of anything, especially his performance. This is slacker heaven, mecca, and nirvana, all wrapped into one. What did Slick Leonard of the Pacer's say everytime Reggie made a three, "Boom Baby!"

Allow me to further describe Bub. What follows are only a few examples, yet I think you will get the picture. Come in late, and do it often. We were to arrive at eight in the morning, not 8:30, 9:00, 10:30, or whenever you slacker well please. Come in late, say around 11:30 and then immediately go to lunch. Use your wife and kids as an excuse for every time you are late or need to leave early, or when you aren't coming in at all.

When you do become a manager, find out what your direct reports are making, and what package they negotiated, and "rip" them for negotiating so well.

If your subordinates ever decide to emulate your behavior, make sure you hold them accountable to standards that you yourself don't keep. Hypocracy, Bub? No.

On another note, Bub didn't handle stress very well. When he got stressed, he got angry. When he was angry he got stressed. When he was angry and stressed, he took it out on his subordinates. Point that finger, point it fast, and blame, blame, blame! He once told us that when things go well he gives us the credit, but when things go bad, he takes the credit. Uh, that never happened.

On another day, Bub assigned me to handle a project and get it ready for review and test, but I wasn't to look at the product, or become familiar with it, because it might bias my judgement. I know I'm dense, but I still don't understand that one.

So, in order to get our work done, we had to ignore him most of the time and just do what we thought was right. See, he was promoted to a management position, but had never had any training in management, and was never given any afterwards. True slacker companies never train managers. If they do, it's only on the legal aspects of managing employees. They don't want to get sued, but if they would have their managers manage their people from a human perspective, then maybe they wouldn't get sued in the first place.

I know we all like to bash people in marketing, but have you ever reported to someone that had a technical background like Bub? If you have, then you know exactly what I mean, marketing is nothing compared to reporting to engineers. Most technical folks, especially engineers, went to school to design and develop products, not manage people. They only go into management because as they move up the ladder there is no other place to go.

Bub in his office with the door closed taking a snooze.

Upper Management and Meetings –

Upper management has some of the best slackers around. They also come up with the best excuses for what they do. Some managers think they are much more important to the future of their company than the subordinates that report to them, emphasis on subordinates, and these same managers go to great lengths to perfect their skills. They hide their insecurities behind the position and power they hold. I believe many of them have taken drama classes, for their ability to pretend with so much determination, emotion, and seriousness, is unsurpassed. They honestly believe they are genetically superior.

Many managers attend meetings every day and all day. Most of the meetings at my old firm were not worth much. They were without agendas, time frames, and a procedure for utilizing an individual's time. Remember, with written agendas and time frames, managers would be held accountable to some sort of standard. Accountability is the worst enemy of a slacker, or at least a manager pretending to be just that, a manager.

The meetings I observed were designed to keep the manager in the limelight. The graphs, charts, and verbiage used were all designed to make the manager look great in his own eyes. What does my father-in-law say, "They were a legend in their own mind."

Many managers and or slackers use meetings to improve their own standing among their peers. They use it to boost their egos, and they believe the visibility will enhance their ability to move up the corporate ladder to more lucrative duties. In many cases they're right. The bigger the slacker, the more time wasted, the more worthless the information, the faster he moves up the ladder. The "Peter Principle" definitely applies here.

With so many slackers in control of so many firms, it's a wonder anything productive ever gets done. I digress. I am here to espouse the mind and life style of the slacker, not just impugn them.

You've Got to be Kidding –

I was working as a consultant with a firm that did commissioning. Commissioning is verifying the equipment you have ordered matches your invoice. The firm we were working for had decided that when filling out documentation, you were only allowed to use Black ink. No Blue ink would be acceptable. That would have been nice to know ahead of time.

In a typical compliance environment, Blue or Black ink is just fine. It just doesn't matter to them what color you use just as long as you use Blue or Black. Red is not allowed. It causes too many questions and problems. It implies something is wrong. Now being the slacker that I am, I was using Blue ink, mainly because Bub always wanted me to use Black. Now not just any Black pen. I was to use a special "validation pen" that had a specific fine tip that Bub approved and no other pen would do. Anal maybe? So I used a Blue pen when off-site at the client's site. Remember, Blue is totally acceptable for any compliance related facility. In my entire career, I cannot point to even one instance, other than this one, where a company had a problem with Blue ink. They shouldn't because it doesn't matter! Yet there are always those out there that know better.

So, I filled out the test data in Blue ink. By the time I was done, there must have been 400 pages of data. The Commissioning manager approached me and let me know I should have used Black ink. As stated before, I sure didn't know that to begin with, and if I had, I would have used Black. I suggested, in order to make the Commissioning documents look professional, to reprint all of the pages, and since I was the one that did the work in the first place, re-enter the data in Black. No he said, that would compromise the integrity of the data. I was to cross-through each data entry, enter my initials and date each correction. I was then to re-enter the data in Black ink. You've got to be kidding I said. He said no I'm not. So some 4 million hours later, not really, some 4 – 6 hours later, the corrections were made and it improved absolutely nothing. He sat with me the entire time to make sure I did it right. So between us, a total of 8 -12 hours was wasted. Wow.

Have you heard about "enough and too much." This was definitely one of those moments where this activity was way too much. Being able to distinguish the important from the un-important is crucial for any manager, and for that matter, any slacker. If you lack the ability to distinguish, you really need to get some training. What a total waste of time. The process set up by the client was wrong to begin with, and making me cross-through and correct each entry was just sad. Why would you punish a slacker in such a manner? Slackers really get irritated when they have to repeat work that adds no value.

More of Bub –

Those that despise people will never get the best out of others and themselves. Alexis De Tocqueville

I think you can agree that Bub was very special. In my humble opinion, he was arrogant, defensive, backstabbing, and attacking all in one. As I look back on my career in working with him, I was angry at the way I was abused and sad for him at the same time. He got along just fine with those laterally and above, but look out if you were below or reported to him. What follows are some more examples on how Bub and I interacted and for that matter how Bub would interact with others.

Slacker Bub at times would imply that you are incompetent and keep you constantly on the defensive. He would never judge any direct reports by their actual Goals and Objectives, even if all were met early or on time. He used the company bonus system as a punishment mechanism and felt gratification in doing so. Even if you had legitimately earned your entire bonus, he would keep a large portion of it back to punish you. He ruled with an iron fist and communicated with a hammer.

Let me know how often you would like to meet one-on-one? Me - Oh, I really don't need much contact, in fact, if you just let me do my job and leave me alone to do my work I would be happy. I will contact you whenever I need you especially when fighting fires. So, if we meet once or twice a year that's fine. Bub, Okay, we will meet every week; week one as a team, and week two one-on-one, and we will do this every other week forever.

We started meeting every week 1-on-1 yet no one else in my department did. The department meeting schedule stayed at every-other week. Every four weeks, I now met with Bub 6 times a month. He said it was so we could spend more time together and work on my "development." He wanted me to believe I was broken and needed fixed. I would have my doctor do a complete physical, but nothing out of the ordinary would be found; blood work, urinalysis, anal exams, nothing. I would look in the mirror for hours on end doing a health self-examination, and still nothing. What could the issues be? Maybe you have an idea?

Summer hours – Basic rules, if you work four 10-hour days, you can take off the next workday as a Summer Day. Bub's rules - You must work 1 hour over each day for a total of 8 hours prior to taking a day off. You cannot take a summer day off before you take off the following week for vacation. Counting individual hours or half hours and totaling them up is not allowed. What? How else would you do it then? All hours must be accumulated prior to actually taking the day off. If you so choose, you can use a summer day in place of a vacation day. By the time he was done with this, I was thoroughly confused. He made rules on the fly and they changed often.

Abusive Managers and My Opinion –

Please let me throw stones and be critical before I even try to understand what's going on, that's just the way I operate. Everything, I mean everything, should be the same criticality. Everything is at risk and I will not tolerate anyone disagreeing with me. No one should be comfortable in their job and I am the one to see to it that they are not. I am me! Everything should be a crisis.

Whenever things don't go perfectly, even if you are not to blame, blaming you is what I will do. I will become visibly irritated, frustrated, constipated (where's my Activia) and in your face. I will blame you and put you on the defensive. That is what I do best. I will question you, question your integrity, intelligence, and believe everyone else before I ever believe you. I am me and I reign supreme! Yes, I will do this in private and in department meetings. I intend to intimidate anyone at any time. I am me! Oh by the way, I don't get stressed. Oh, and considering you, I don't think it has to do with competence, or does it? Are you incompetent?

Let's step back for a moment, as a rule, we know people learn from their mistakes, but once corporate America has it in for you, the next opportunity they have, you are gone. They do not care that you have proven yourself, you're gone.

The motto of abusive managers, Bub included - remember, this is my book, so I at least get to tell you how I felt, if chicken soup is good for the soul, can whining be good as well? Anyway, here it is – I cannot be responsible to my employees because I do not consider them as an individual nor do I respect them. I do not respect their dignity or recognize their merit. They are nothing but expendable resources and should be thought of as such. Security in a job should be considered a relic of the past. None of my subordinates, emphasis on subordinates, should feel secure. Whether they stay employed or not is not based on their performance, but on my personal whims. Subordinates freely offering suggestions and complaints, whom are you kidding? Subordinates are just a bunch of whiners. No one should listen to them. Development and advancement will be up to me, if they don't like it, they can leave. What is competent management? I am competent management because I am me. All of my actions are just and ethical in my own eyes. I am not and will not be judged by anyone but myself. There is no higher power than me. I am god!

Wow, I'm painting a very negative picture here aren't I? I try to be as honest as I can. Is this my point of view, sure it is. Is it correct? Of course it is, this my book.

Here are some more insane statements and situations from abusive mangers to pass your way –

I will schedule meetings and then not show up. I will accept other meeting invitations, and always show up late. People should cater to me. I do not cater to anyone. I am the manager!

If there is an issue I do not agree with, or if the truth were told, I do not understand, I will cover myself by blaming others, and especially my direct reports. If need be, I will go over the heads of others in order to make them look bad and ruin their reputation. I am me! I am the manager!

Oh, I need you to configure Outlook so that I can see your daily schedule and then judge whether you are using your time appropriately. Oh that's right, I decide what is appropriate.

Bub - I want you to start using a new tool instead of the Excel file you are using for our department inventory list. I do not agree with you that there are limitations. I know I have never used the tool or the Excel file. You will use the new tool even though Excel is more powerful and easier to use. Me - the old phrase applies "Don't confuse me with the facts, my mind is made up."

In speaking with Bub, it soon became apparent that I was to just sit there and be quite, nod my heard and do as I was told. I was to be a Gary bobble-head. My new approach, in as much as possible, was to speak only when spoken to and add nothing. Just bobble, bobble, bobble, bobble, bobble, bobble, bobble....

Miscommunication from Bub on an email he sent out. Out of the blue, Bub said he no longer wanted to talk to me using email. Could this be true? Could it be that my prayers had been answered? Could it actually be that this form of communication was off-limits? Eureka! Oh happy day! ♫ Oh What a Beautiful Morning, Oh What a Beautiful Day, I Have a Wonderful Feeling, Everything's Going My Way. ♫ All of his would have been great if he really meant it. I never wanted to talk to him ever. Not in person, not on the phone, and certainly not by email. He didn't keep his word. He continued to talk to me by email. Rats! I was slowly being driven nuts.

Side note on "perception" – Hopefully your perception is based on truth and not the other way around. We only see our co-workers from one perspective and we should not judge their entire character based on what we see or what we think we see. I believe the following is from Steven Covey, he tells of a man that gets on a city bus with four small children. All of the children are misbehaving, hair unwashed, etc. The man is unshaved, disheveled and seems to be drunk. He just isn't doing well. A woman follows them onto the bus. Her perception is that he is a terrible father and a drunk. After a few minutes of this, she loses her temper and says that he needs to control his kids and even threatens him with child protective services. Like the government does anything well, other than the Military? The man looks up and says

I'm sorry about my kids; I'm going through some rough times right now. You see, my wife had cancer for the past six months and she passed away yesterday, so please forgive me, things have not been good.

Her perception, he was a terrible father and a drunk. The truth, he was actually a great Dad and he wasn't drunk, just really depressed. The old phrase "Don't judge a book by its cover" still applies to many situations.

In passing one day, I heard that HR had outsourced some of their work to a local company where a friend of mine Marvin worked. He used to work for the same firm I did. I said to Bub, isn't it funny how things work out? Marvin is now kind of back on the payroll. Do you remember the song, "Back in the Saddle Again" by Gene Autry? This is not the Aerosmith version. It's the version from the 30s. Sing it as ♫ I'm Back on the Payroll Again, I'm Back on the Payroll Again, I'm Back on the Payroll Again. ♫ There is nothing wrong with that statement, "back on the payroll." Bub said the name of Marvin offended him and that I was never to mention his name at work ever again.

I was asked to send out an email on standard policies, procedures, and forms to all in our department. This is what they were to use for the future. Bub sent an email asking if I had received any questions concerning what I sent out. I replied "no." He said, "you don't understand, did you receive any questions", I said "no." He asked again, and again I responded with no. He responded with (?) I replied no, but that one employee had asked if we had any templates (examples), so I did create three. I sent them to him and told Bub this. He said COME TO MY OFFICE! Once there He said, you BUFFON (he didn't really say that, but that is what I heard) you don't understand me, did you receive any questions concerning this, I said no. How many more times can I say no to this? He said. Do you know if they understood from your email that they needed to use these templates? I said, I don't know. There were no questions and that is what I told them to use for the future. He said I find it strange that you don't find it strange that no one had any questions. I wanted to answer with I find it strange, that you find it strange that I don't find it strange that no one had any questions!

Another conversation with Bub - He told me I needed to be more cynical yet on another week told me that I needed to be less negative. We discussed the differences between cynical and negative. I've got to ask, isn't this book cynical and negative? Cynical and negative is a very big part of my life. He was talking to an expert in the field and didn't even know it. How could he, he was the all-knowing, all-powerful Bub!

Bub started to review every word I put in an email and every word I put in meeting invitations. He then complained how I worded things. He constantly said that I wasn't "managerial." If managerial means treating direct reports like garbage, then count me non-managerial. Managerial in my definition is treating others with respect, trusting them to do their job, not micro managing them, and definitely practicing character and integrity.

Maybe he was irritated with me as a living breathing human being, and also a Manager, I don't know. He was unhappy with everything. I'm sure it had to do with some huge void in his life so he took it out on me and others. He really needed help and fast. I was not equipped to help him with his many apparent behavioral issues.

When you hire people and put them into positions of leadership, the first criteria should be that they have the skills to lead. Do you understand? It should not be based on race, color, creed, or diversity. It has to be based on ability. It should not matter if they are a man or a woman. Leaders must be able to lead.

At my last performance review, Bub acted as prosecuting attorney, judge, and jury. He manipulated my review to say exactly what he wanted it to say. I think you can guess if it were positive or negative. A sizable chunk of my bonus was withheld.

Now if you were to take anything from me in the non-corporate world, you could end up being arrested, but not if it's done within the walls of corporate America where bonuses are concerned. On one hand, they use them as a carrot to get you to jump and on the other, a club to punish. Now to be fair, bonuses are also used to reward solid performance. It really depends on where you work and to whom you report. But never underestimate the inerrant behavior of hateful bosses.

I was done with Bub. I had endured him year after year after year. No longer could I put up with him. I was being driven nuts and this had to stop before I actually did go nuts. My patience and perseverance were stretched beyond its limits. I decided to leave and turned in my resignation.

Now sometimes there is just nothing you can do with the circumstances you find yourself in. Sometimes the best you can do is the best you can do. Take Shadrach, Meshach and Abednego, Daniel, Joseph, Stephen, Esther, and most of the disciples, they were confronted with problems I could never even dream of, yet they persevered and I am striving to do so as well.

If I ever feel that my latest job isn't going well, I just read these pages about Bub and suddenly everything is back in perspective. I'm not the one that was broken, Bub was, and he desperately needed help.

The sad thing is, the company I worked for was and still is a great company. People do not leave companies they leave people. It's difficult for HR departments and even managers to know exactly what is going on with their employees. HR will have exit interviews but they are merely just an exercise in futility and nothing more. They asked what my relationship was with Bub and I told them that it was straight out of a nightmare. I said that Bub is a bully and that this behavior will repeat itself. Bullies have to have someone to pick on. Give it six to eight months and he will be at this again.

Pink Floyd has a song entitled "Brain Damage" I encourage you to listen to it some time. It really fits my experience with Bub. The lyrics go as follows:

"The lunatic is on the grass
The lunatic is on the grass
Remembering games and daisy chains and laughs
Got to keep the loonies on the path
The lunatic is in the hall
The lunatics are in my hall
The paper holds their folded faces to the floor
And every day the paper boy brings more
And if the dam breaks open many years too soon
And if there is no room upon the hill
And if your head explodes with dark forbodings too
I'll see you on the dark side of the moon
The lunatic is in my head
The lunatic is in my head
You raise the blade, you make the change
You re-arrange me 'till I'm sane
You lock the door
And throw away the key
There's someone in my head but it's not me.
And if the cloud bursts, thunder in your ear
You shout and no one seems to hear
And if the band you're in starts playing different tunes
I'll see you on the dark side of the moon."

I think of him from time to time. I still hold a lot of bitterness and resentment, but that is something I'm working on. I just pray and hope that God will get hold of him someday, shake his fear and arrogance down to its foundation, and rebuild him in His image. He really needs the Lord.

Diversity –

Even though I haven't specifically talked about this previously, I want to talk about Diversity. Is Diversity a good thing? Yes, if used for the right reasons. You shouldn't be put in a position of leadership because of your race, color, creed, or sex. You should be put in a position of leadership because you are qualified to lead.

Many companies these days are more concerned with numbers and in meeting "Diversity goals" than they are in putting good people in positions that they deserve. Since when do quotas ensure anything but some sort of discrimination? Be it regular discrimination or reverse discrimination, either way, its discrimination. You should only be put in management positions based on qualifications and past work experience. You say that's easy for me to say because I'm a white male and I'm already in the "privileged club." You're the one reading my book. What privileged clubs have I belonged to? If I have been given any breaks at all it wasn't because of whom I knew or where I found myself. In fact, it has been quite the opposite. I have been successful through hard work and a tremendous amount of slacking uh, I mean perseverance. No games, no favors, just working within the system and doing my best to practice character and integrity along the way.

I have seen people put in positions of leadership that they simply didn't deserve, and I am sure you have as well. Then what you get is someone in way over their head and thinking that they really deserve to be where they are. They quite often develop arrogance and overriding pride and believe they got the position based on their own merit. They didn't. Quite often, they got there based on other "attributes" rather than qualifications. Then the whole work group suffers because the corporation was more concerned with Diversity numbers than in identifying good leaders.

You think it is tough being you because of your race, color, creed, sex, or maybe even sexual orientation, so you deserve special treatment? Try being a Christian in corporate America. Tell me how that turns out? We have actual bigots in this country. We have degree bigots, and we have religious bigots. In addition, most of the religious bigots are generally bigoted towards Christians. Wow, I digress.

Do yourself a favor and identify strong leadership potential in your people, not because of their race, color, creed, or sex, but because they are the most qualified for the position. Your company will be better for it and so will the leaders you have identified.

Chapter 3: Suggestions and Comments

You're probably thinking that I have criticized a lot of individuals within these few short pages, mainly Bub, and you're right, I have. You're probably also asking yourself, if I'm so slacker brilliant then why don't I offer some alternatives or solutions. Okay, I will. They're all fairly simplistic. Life doesn't have to be as hard as we make it. Life and work can and should be fun.

1) Stop playing corporate games. Stop the political ploys. Do what's right because it's the right thing to do. Things are not as gray as you would always like them to be. They are generally as black and white as night and day. If you truly do not know the difference between right and wrong, ask and seek help. You should pray for wisdom and discernment. The God of Abraham, Isaac, and Jacob will help you. Make sure you close in Jesus name. You want the prayer to get there.

2) Don't latch on to each new business method that comes your way. It will save you a lot of money if you don't. Do a little research. Ask, do they work, and if so where? Seek out those companies that implemented them and ask what went well and what didn't? Ask them if they would utilize those methods again?

3) Use the brain that God gave you. Common sense should rule the day. Don't make things more difficult than they need to be. If it doesn't add value, then don't do it. Ask yourself as a manager, if you would do the thing(s) you are asking of your subordinates? Would you do it if you were

in the same position as them, and if not, then why are you having them do it? Please don't tell me, "I am asking them to do it because it's beneath me and in my lofty position, I don't do those things." Could arrogance and pride be preventing you?

4) Spend corporate money and resources as if they were your own. Don't waste dollars simply because you can. Don't hire additional employees unless they are needed.

5) When you send subordinates to training, let them utilize the training when they get back. Don't just use it as a "check-off."

6) Managers, stop being so arrogant. You do make mistakes. Apologize occasionally. You will find that it takes more strength and courage to apologize than it does to remain quiet. Embrace your mistakes and learn from them. Remember, Pride goes before a fall and a little humility goes a long way.

7) When doing yearly reviews, tell the truth. Don't play games. It's already stressful enough for the employee; they don't need you to play the BIG ME, little you game. Just tell the truth about their performance, and if you don't know, then use the 360 we talked about earlier. They're not hard to do. Link the review to the yearly increase (COL) and merit pay. Why? Because you should.

8) When new on the job, learn the environment and develop relationships with your employees and co-workers before making suggestions (criticizing). Offer help on content not format. Do you know how angry and frustrated you make subordinates when you want change for the sake of

change? It has been stated "Change for the sake of change is not progress, but stupidity." Get real. Get smart.

9) Practice the Golden Rule. You know it; "Do unto others as you would have them do unto you." It's not do unto others simply because you can. Do you not know that God will hold you accountable? You have an obligation and a responsibility to act in a professional manner, so why don't you do it? God has blessed you by putting you in the position you're in; don't blow it.

Affirmation –

I was talking with a co-worker one day and he described to me how his outlook and attitude about work had changed recently. He said, Gary, I used to come to work with a good attitude. I liked being here, I enjoyed my job, and even if I needed to stay longer to finish my work, I never minded. Now, since I started reporting to my new manager, I dread Mondays terribly. I don't really lose sleep like so many others do, worrying about going back to work on Monday, every Sunday evening I just get physically ill. I don't enjoy my work anymore and I just hate being there, and it's all because of my new manager. I am stuck between a rock and a hard place. We have too few people to get the job done, and too few hours to do it. So I get blamed when we miss deadlines, and there is nothing I can do about it.

I told my friend that when you're put in that type of situation, sometimes the best you can do is just to do your best. Either put up with it, fight to change it, or look for another job.

Of the many years that I have worked in corporate America, I have seen a number of managers come and go. Many seemed to have trouble with character and integrity. Most did not deserve the position that they had been handed nor had they earned it. They did not govern with professionalism, nor did they respect their direct reports. Just because you have obtained a lofty position does not validate that you deserve to be there. Respect must be earned; it is never just given.

I think most of you will agree that with any new boss, the jury is out until a few weeks or so to see how they govern and how they treat you and others. Just because a manager is successful in meeting the goals and objectives of the organization, that, in and of itself, does not make them successful. It all depends on what you consider successful. I consider success as meeting the company's goals and objectives by building the best team possible, training them well, and then supporting them in doing so. Anyone can govern with an iron fist and communicate with a hammer. Actually leading by example and respecting your employees is another thing all together.

If you have a track record, like me, in dealing with someone like Bub, I encourage you to find a "foundational" company. If possible, find a company that pays well, offers great benefits, a bonus perhaps, and good vacation. If you have to put up with the abuse and insanity, you might as well be paid well for it.

Am I always happy with the management I report to, no, but what else can you do? You have to do your best to get along with difficult people. Influence and change what you can and always count your blessings. You have to sort out the good with the bad, and hopefully there is more good than bad.

We are in a battle of sorts, for our sanity, our self-respect, and for our dignity, so don't give up, don't give in, and never surrender. You want to flourish not just survive.

I hope you're not just surviving. If so, that's really sad. It bothers me that so many of us are put in "surviving" situations. I think I can argue that most of these situations, either being abused by a manager, or living in a situation that is poorly managed, is a direct result of companies putting non-qualified managers in those positions. I feel for all of you and wish things were different. I know they can be. It's going to take time and a lot of effort. Upper management needs to get a clue and help, and employees need to push back to get their H.R. departments to implement the 360-degree review process I talked about earlier. They need to ensure that it adequately addresses the performance of each manager. They then need to provide training, support, and consequences to actions that are less than expected. Simply stated, if managers refuse to start acting with character and integrity, and treating their employees with respect, then they need to be forced to seek opportunities elsewhere.

We live in the greatest nation on earth, and quite possibly the greatest nation the world has ever known, and look how we act and treat each other. It's truly a shame.

Please keep in mind that people do not leave companies, they leave people. Think about it, in the jobs that you have left, it most likely was not because of low pay or benefits, because most companies compete very well with that. You left because you didn't get along with your supervisor and/or were being abused by him. You left because you didn't think the problems would change for the better in either the short-term or the long-term.

If you consider the Bible for a moment, it talks about being the "body of Christ." Meaning, the foot cannot tell the hand I don't need you anymore than the hand can tell the head I don't need you. If as Christians, we are all part of the body and we all contribute to life through our various talents and gifts. In the same way, we, meaning you and me, are all part of the company. The company is not made of buildings and equipment it's made up of you and me, for without the employee there is no company. We need to respect each other no matter what our position in life, because we all add value in some way or another.

If you have ever been involved in similar situations as these, or dealt with people such as those discussed here, I sympathize with you. You know when you've done a good job, and you know when you've been singled out and been mistreated. You also know an abuse of power when confronted with it. Are all managers and supervisors bad, no, but for a large number, wow!

I leave you with this thought, "Put on the full armor of God so that you can take your stand against the devil's schemes." "For our struggle is not against flesh and blood, but against the rulers, against the authorities, against the powers of this dark world and against the spiritual forces of evil in the heavenly realms." Ephesians 6:11-12.

Slacker Stories -

Chapter 4: Slackers

Jabba the Hut –

I remember one slacker that worked in my company. He reminded me a lot of "Star Wars Jabba the Hut." He was massive. He really resembled a huge bowling ball, kind of like a "Weeble." He was bald and round, and when he laughed, his belly shook like a bowl of jelly. Well, not really.

He would sit on his lab stool, and raise it as high as it would go. This allowed him to look down on his subordinates, as if a king perched on his throne looking down on all his subjects. He had an attitude kind of like SBD Kevin.

In the seven or so years I knew him, I don't believe I saw him do more than a few hours of work per week. He was a slacker supervisor, and slacker supervisors never perform work. No, no, no, no, no, they obtained their position because they were superior to other slackers. If the others were so talented, then they would be Slacker Jabba.

Jabba had slacked his way to the top; therefore, he had become what my father calls, a "level three," where you have "arrived" and will never have to put in a good 40 hours' worth of work ever again!

Memo's and the Frightened Slacker-

I attended an in-house course on technical writing. It was very good. It taught how to be precise and how to get to the point quickly. Slackers generally never send lengthy memos, except, when needed. One of the attendees, let's call her Slacker Jung, had submitted a memo ahead of time for the instructor to review and use as an example in class. It was a page long in 10-point font; she finally got to the point in the last paragraph. The entire page, I mean the entire page with filled with text. The instructor then asked what was going on with this memo. I replied that the writer didn't know how to answer the person the memo had been addressed to, and didn't want the reader to know she didn't know. Slacker Jung drew offense to my statement and said that she didn't want the person she was writing to, to know she didn't know the answer, because that would make her look dumb. Instead of saying she would get back with him later, when she did find the answer, she tried to dazzle him with her knowledge of the English language.

Slackers always try to cover their tracks and blow smoke wherever they can. Remember, symbolism over substance doesn't work very well. Looking dumb never helps your career, and wasting another's time doesn't help either?

Union Mentality and the Obvious –

My wife used to work for an automotive firm. The union decided that top line pay, vacation, and benefits were not enough for their slacker workforce, so they decided to strike. "We'll show management" was their mantra.

There were approximately 1800 employees at the plant. When they went on strike, the company required 600 salary employees to work 12-hour days for six weeks. Believe it or not, the salaried employees produced just as much product with better quality. Of course the slacker union reps denied this and stated that management was lying. What's the saying, numbers don't lie, but liars do? The other phase is "say a lie long enough and keep repeating it until it soon becomes the truth."

Anyway, the union took it upon themselves to pull a fast one. Before the strike took place, the union built some slick little devices that would hold roofing nails upright. It was a roofing nail through the middle of a Gerber's baby food lid. Isn't it grand what a slacker can do when he puts his mind to it? When my wife drove our car into work one day, she was a salaried employee, they all began shouting profanities at her, diverted her attention, and placed two puncture devices under her right side tires. Two brand new BF Goodrich radial TA's wasted.

With another incident, a summer intern had not been informed of the strike in time, and drove his grandmother's antique Impala to work. The union slackers proceeded to beat the car to a pulp with baseball bats. One slacker was caught on video. The company promptly fired him, but he was a member of the union. The union forced the company to rehire him and pay him back pay; he lost nothing. Unions and slackers, there's no better partnership.

The company had had enough. The union had refused to budge on the major issues, so a large number of union jobs were eventually lost to Mexico. Those union employees were now hard pressed to find a job that would replace the one they had just lost. Only those with education and higher skills could move on and not lose. No thanks should be given to the union reps. Sometimes it's better to lose a little than to lose it all.

Industrial Engineering and the Union –

My wife was working in the I.E. department one week, when she was called upon to run a time study on one of the production lines. Of course, the union was informed well ahead of time so they could "Jimmy" the line speed. They were on a piece-meal system. For instance, if the quota was 75 pieces a shift, and you produced 100, you were paid an additional bonus for the extra 25. They deliberately slowed down the line to produce, let's say 60 pieces, and then hoped my wife would base the study on that line speed. She wasn't that stupid. She has never been a slacker, and being related to me, she was very aware of the tricks slackers' pull.

The Slacker and Personal Hygiene –

There was one slacker who worked in our documentation department; he was a bit weird, even for a slacker. We called him "Larry the Martian." Larry had one peculiar problem that none of us could miss; he very rarely cut his fingernails. Generally slackers try to blend in with the crowd, that way it's easier to slack, and not get caught. Larry the Martian had fingernails that were about two inches long and had begun to curl under. If I were not mistaken, I would swear that he had painted them pink one day.

Slackers, beware, you must blend in, or you will end up like a tall blade of grass or an unwanted weed; you will be cut down at the knees. Larry the Martian never moved up the slacker ladder and neither will you, unless you blend, blend, and blend.

The Triple Dipper –

I went out to lunch with a couple of co-workers the other day. One of the slackers had ordered some cheese sticks. The cheese sticks came with Marinara sauce. He was gracious enough to offer us some. The slacker sitting beside me proceeded to dip his cheese stick into the sauce, that's okay, except he continued to do it after each new bite. I looked at the co-worker across from me, and our eyes met as if to say, did we just see what we think we saw? We did. I looked at the "Triple Dipper" and said, Hey man, did you just triple dip? He said, yes and that he weren't contagious. I said, sure, you may not be contagious, but I wouldn't want to eat after either one of you even if you weren't. He did stop dipping, but only because his cheese-sticks were gone.

Hogs, Beer, and Gas Tanks –

Have you ever noticed that a lot of "Hog" riders drink a lot of beer? You can tell by the size of their large midsections. This is where the gas tank of the bike comes in handy. "Hogs" gas tanks offer a wonderful mechanism to reduce the amount of drop, or hanging if you will, for the belly of the "Hog" rider. Let me explain, The "Hog" rider has his bike on the kickstand, he then places his hands under his belly, lifts it six or eight inches, places his right leg over the bike, and then rests his belly on the tank, that's what the tank is used for. It would be hard for a beer-drinking, slackin, "Hog" of a guy, to ride long distances without some sort of support for that beer belly.

Hog riders also seem to like wearing those helmets that skirt D.O.T. regulations. Slackers may not be all that people think they should be, but you have to admit they do work very hard at ignoring common sense and the law. You've seen them, those little helmets that look like a basketball that has been cut into and placed on their heads, very little padding, and no face shield. It's great to have the wind in your hair and bugs in your teeth. Bugs, tattoos, and black clothing all add a lot to the "Hog" mystique.

Body Shop Slackers –

We once had a group of slackers who came to my hometown and offered to do an entire paint job on your car for $100; too good to be true you ask? It certainly was.

Before I took my car over to be painted, I did a little sanding on my own. I delivered the car to them and they assured me that I really didn't need to do any prep work. They would take care of it all. Believe me, they had no intention of doing any bodywork, and they didn't.

When they called me to pick up the car, not only was no prep work done, but I also had bugs stuck in the paint of my car. The bugs were all over the hood. Little bug hood ornaments. There were also two areas on my car that required you to bend over to paint them (wheel flares) just behind the front wheels. They hadn't bothered with them either. When I informed them of the bugs and the unpainted areas, they flipped the bugs off with their forefinger, and got a rag, dipped it in a can of silver paint, and rubbed it on the areas they missed.

This is pure, pure, "Slackerism." They were only in town about a month and then skipped on out. They were true slackers, and thieves to boot, what a wonderful combination.

Insurance –

I owned a 2000 Pontiac Grand Prix GTP. I was traveling home one day when I was rear-ended from behind. That's like the same thing isn't it? Is that a double negative? I was waiting at a stoplight and when it turned Green I started to take off and a woman in a late model Acura MDX hit me. We both pulled off on the side of the road. She readily admitted she hit me and said the reason why, was that a car rear-ended her on a hit-and-run. We called the police to file a report. The Police said that it wasn't enough damage in their opinion and refused to issue one.

I took a look my rear bumper. It now had quite a few scratches and it was embossed with Acura imbedded in the bumper cover. I looked at her car. Her front bumper sustained no damaged. The rear bumper had a small vertical ½-inch cut, most likely from dropping something when lifting it up and into the back of the vehicle through the lift-gate. Remember, she hit me. I contacted my insurance company and let them know what had happened. They asked, who do you think is a fault here? I replied, she is, she hit me and admitted it. They said we are not going to pay out because it was a hit-and-run. It will have to go on your insurance and you will have to fulfill your deductible first. She had the same insurance company I had. I said, wait a minute, she hit me, and I am not a cartoon, I lack the slacker ability to run around and rear-end myself. They said, doesn't matter, we are not going to pay. I said, you know what, I just walked by 20 cars in the parking lot at work (yes I was at work talking to my insurance company, where else would I be) and 8 out of the 20 all had some sort of blemish on their back bumpers. Was it all due to a hit-and-run? They replied don't know. I replied, then how can you say she hit me via a hit-and-run from a small cut in her bumper? They said it doesn't matter, we believe it was a hit-and-run and we are not going to pay out on a claim just to keep a customer. I asked what if you were my insurance company, and she was insured by a competitor and was still claiming it was a hit-and-run? They said we would then litigate. Isn't that great?

I informed them that after my youngest daughter started driving, that they would be getting close to $40,000 dollars from me in premiums over the next few years, and they were worried about not paying out on a $486.00 claim. Wow, is that not penny wise and pound-foolish? I cancelled my insurance and found another company with the same coverage for $700.00 less per year. Their motto found on many bumper stickers and billboards, "Premiums Are Us - We Collect, You Pay."

I called up the state insurance commission to tell them about the slacker company I was working with and they said they couldn't help me. It was all up to the insurance company to decide. Man, is that not a waste of time or what? Why do we even have a state insurance commission if the companies have lobbied so well that the law means nothing?

So next time you hit someone just claim you were hit from behind by a slacker via a hit-and-run. Apparently any scratch or blemish will do.

Consumer Updates –

I owned a 1992 Pontiac Transport GT mini-van. Its exterior was made of 100% SMC (sheet-molded compound) or plastic. Shortly after I purchased the van, I was reading a well-known consumer's magazine, and I noticed that they said the Toyota Previa's "body exterior (rust)" was better than average. Meaning, it didn't rust very much. Yet, my van was "body exterior (rust)" was below average? I found this was very interesting. I wrote to them and pointed out this little discrepancy. They wrote back and informed me that they would pass it on to the appropriate department and offered me a discount to continue my subscription. I declined.

Folks, my van could not rust even if you wanted it to. You could strip the paint clean, shoot the body full of holes and it will not rust, ever! So how is the "body exterior (rust)" below average? Please, oh great and powerful consumer magazine, help me understand this?

The Guarantee –

My father-in-law purchased a new kitchen faucet the other day. It was quite nice. It had your basic faucet with the sprayer and all. The warranty was quite interesting; it stated, "It was guaranteed for its full useful life." What's up with that? Some slacker lawyer must have had a hey-day with that statement. Useful life, is this one-day, two days, three days, four, five days, six days, or seven days more?

The Herd –

Back at the one firm I use to work for, smokers were required to smoke outside; like so many other companies nowadays. It was always so interesting to see them go out to take a smoke in 95-degree heat, and even when it was ten degrees below zero. They would all congregate in front of the main entrance. They resembled a herd of cattle mingling under a tree to get out of the rain.

How can you be so devoted, or so addicted, as to subject yourself to such torture? The snow/wind could be blowing at 30 mph, and they would still smoke. The sun could be so hot that you could burn yourself by just touching the hood of your car. Yet they still smoked.

Since they were always blocking the entrance while smoking, I always felt like I was running a gauntlet just to enter the building. The herd just never got out of the way.

CEO's Pay –

Much has been said in the media about the pay and benefits that CEOs receive. My Dad says they are Level 3. That is where they have reached their "perch" because of the many years they have dedicated to slacking. You don't earn 4 million bucks a year with stock options to boot, just because you worked hard. Think about it. Who else can get a fat cat raise while their company is losing money? You and I can't, but fat cat slackers can. Who else can get millions in utilizing their stock options while being let go to "pursue opportunities elsewhere"?

At the firm I worked for, we had one VP that was fired. They gave him a "golden handshake" (salary to last one year) with a secretary and an off-site office all to help him find a new job. Now figure this, you get fired, get a 1-year's severance package, and off site office and a secretary? This was a piece of Slacker Heaven! We should give him a big applause and high five at his ability to negotiate such a wonderful package!

A large grocery store chain's CEO put the company into bankruptcy and was offered a couple of million dollars to stay and help them out of it. Wow, he puts them into bankruptcy and is rewarded for it? As a slacker I can't even dream of something that good.

A few years back, a home improvement store forced their CEO out, and gave him 230 million to leave. Please let me regain my composure for a minute

. . . .

. . . .

. . . . .230 million! He then was hired by an automotive firm to run their operations. Did he have any experience, education, passion or background in automotive? No. If you or I attempted to work there you can bet that we would have to have the experience they are looking for, but for CEOs, nope, nada, nothing, not needed.

What on earth are we doing in American business? If you or I lose millions, or even less, and don't do well in our job for any length of time, we're fired. They like to say laid-off but come on you're fired. That's exactly what it is and we aren't given a few million to stay or go. CEO's earning 365 times the pay of the average American worker is just insane.

Things need to change here. CEOs, Presidents, and VPs are not gods and shouldn't be treated as such. Yes, they have a lot of responsibility and pressure, and they are rewarded for it handsomely. Most of them can retire after only one stint with a major corporation here in America, the rest of us, not so. When will we hold our leaders accountable for their mistakes and stop rewarding them for their failures?

CEO's are the ultimate slackers. While the grunt slackers are actually producing for the company, and being paid relatively little in comparison, the fat cat slackers are planning the next wave of layoffs, buyouts, and reduction in benefits. I guess they need the extra savings in order to buy that new Lexus LFA for their third wife.

Star Wars –

Have you ever worked for an electronics firm, one that builds circuit boards? Well, the guys I worked with told me an interesting story the other day. They used to work in production and told the story of how a co-slacker used to make "Star Wars" figurines out of solder. That's the stuff you attach components to a circuit board with. I understand he was pretty good at it. He would sculpt figurines of "R2D2" "CP3O" "Chewbacca" and the "Millennium Falcon."

This fellow belongs in the Slacker Hall of Fame, although we don't have a Slacker Hall of Fame. We wouldn't have the energy to raise the funds to build it. We certainly wouldn't lift a finger to build it ourselves, because that would require effort. I'm not even sure a slacker knows what effort is. I don't think it's found in the slacker dictionary. Where is that anyway? The Slacker Hall of Fame will just have to stay a pipe dream. Think about it for a moment. Who do you think should be in it? I'm sure you could name a number of slackers you have worked for and with. If you slack really hard, you just might find a bust of yourself in a corner of the Slacker Hall of Fame someday.

List those you think should be in the Slacker Hall of Fame. For example, Relatives, Politicians, Political Parties, Presidents, Teachers, Rock and Roll Stars, Sports Figures, and last and maybe least, your Boss.

1)_____
2)_____
3)_____
4)_____
5)_____
6)_____
7)_____
8)_____
9)_____
10)_____

WSLK –

WSLK are the call letters of a slacker radio station that refused to take a stand. Slackers never take a stand. If they do, they stand somewhere in the middle of the road and take the risk of being run over. For they don't stand for anything, thus they stand for nothing; thus the definition of a slacker.

WSLK had recently pulled a well-known religious speaker and family advocate off the air. I wrote them asking why. The explanation they gave me was pure "Slackerism." It seems that the speaker had talked about politics and the upcoming presidential election. He talked about issues that concerned Christians. He did not tell them how to vote; he merely informed them where the candidates stood on different issues and how they had voted in the past. Kind of like what the "Christian Coalition" has been doing for years, telling the truth.

The radio station took the position that they didn't want their listeners being informed on family issues, especially if it sounded remotely controversial. The radio station pulled the speaker off their airwaves. Keep in mind, the radio station was backed by a well-known Christian college, and was supposed to be a "Christian Radio Station." Yet when I called to challenge them on their decision, I was informed that they were not a Christian radio station they were a radio station that played Christian music. Isn't that's great, slackers that find a niche and present themselves on the air as one thing, but privately as another. This is a real shame. Even if you are a slacker, you should not tempt God. "The Fear of the Lord is the beginning of Wisdom." Proverbs 9:10

Teacher's Unions and Associations –

The public school system in which my children were supposed to attend had some very peculiar ways of teaching and some insidious philosophies. I'm sorry, I should be more understanding, but when it affects the wellbeing and future of my children, I expect others to do their job and do it well. Slackers always expect others to do their best, but never expect the same out of themselves.

They had recently released their standards on how they were going to teach now and in the future. The standards were their math and literacy standards. Now I'm no teacher, and I don't know Jack Kennedy, but I know slacking when I see it. I can also spell potatoe. Their math standards no longer wanted to have "rote memorization of the multiplication tables," and no longer teach, "Any pencil paper computation when it came to long division." You ask why, because of the availability of calculators. If you start a child in kindergarten using calculators and he will never need math basics again. Now what happens if the batteries in their calculator go belly up, or the child doesn't have access to one? Slackers don't really think too far in the future. It hurts to think too deeply.

The literacy standards no longer wanted to teach phonics. Why, because of "See and Say" or "Invented Spelling." What is Invented Spelling you ask? It's exactly how it sounds. Spell it the way you think the word sounds, and don't correct a child until the third grade, because it might hurt their self-esteem.

I found out about Invented Spelling from a drawing my daughter came home with one day after school. She was in kindergarten at the time. She had drawn a picture of a bus. The statement she wrote under the bus said "I lk to rd on the sl bs." (I like to ride on the school bus.) Pretty good for a kindergartner, but they had no intention of correcting her. In fact, they taught her to spell the words exactly the way you read them. Maybe I should say, thy tght her to spl the wds extly the way u rd thm.

They originally wanted to practice invented spelling from K through 12th grade. Incredible! Just show-up at the school and teach nothing. Collect your paycheck, benefits and pension and laugh all the way to the bank.

There was a federal report that came out entitled, SCANS (Secretary of Labor's Commission on Achieving Necessary Skills). The National Association of Slackers, along with the Slackers Federation of Teachers, adopted the commission report on Outcome Based Education and teaching methods.

It was Outcome Based Education, and in theory it should work, and it works exceedingly well for slackers. They wanted to provide multiple opportunities for children to pass the same test. They were to work in groups and receive group grades, with no true accountability. In fact, the SCANS report wanted to eliminate tests, grades, and in some corners of the debate, textbooks. They stated that tests unfairly pit students against one another and grades might label them as smart and dumb. In addition, they stated that it should no longer be pass/fail, but ready try again. Sure, life is about ready, try again, but there are deadlines in life and consequences when we don't meet them. These methods are preparing our students to be the best slackers in the world. "Today's Students, Tomorrow's Slackers."

Another method of keeping parents off the backs of teachers is talking about closing and consolidating facilities. This keeps the parents in an uproar over "sentimentalism," over the building they graduated from, and prevents them from looking at the real issues concerning education. Administrators always have a way of deflecting parent's concerns to other less important subjects, and you should too. Does this sound like political campaigns?

In Indiana, they have the kids take a test every year. It's called, ISTEP. It's designed to access the performance of the students at various grade levels. Unfortunately, for parents and students, and fortunately for teachers, it's a test for Indiana students only. Other states have these too, but you cannot compare the student's performance to any other state in the country.

This is great for your average slacker. No accountability, no comparisons, and if you're a parent and want to do something about it, or something about a bad teacher, try taking on a teacher with tenure and the teacher unions! Just remember Wisconsin, Good Luck!

Disclaimer: Not all teachers are slackers. Some are trying to do a good job amidst a bad situation. Good parents all across America applaud you for your perseverance, determination, and dedication. You know exactly who you are, thanks.

If you know anything about Hoosier basketball, you know one thing; losing is not an option. There is nothing else on earth like Hoosier basketball. The greatest game that was ever invented, the Big O, Miller, Keller, Big Mac, Bird, the Pacers, and Bobby. I'm actually talking about high-school ball though, not professional.

We had one coach that was on the verge of having the distinction of holding the longest losing streak in the state. We were zero and thirty-three. One more loss and we were in the record books.

This coach, Coach Bob, really didn't grasp the fundamentals on how to motivate high school athletes. Consequently, many of the best players refused to play for him.

I was in the journalism club at the time and was asked to write an article on the upcoming season. Try to write an upbeat article on a team that hadn't won a game in nearly two seasons and no returning player that had any talent, it's not easy.

Being a slacker, and seeing how pitiful we were, I decided to go out for the team. I was a junior at the time. I skipped the early season conditioning, as any slacker would, and went out after the beginning of the school year. Keep in mind, I had played against many of the varsity at lunch breaks, and although I wasn't the best of the best, I was very able to play competitively against many of them. I went to my one and only scrimmage and made a few mistakes, i.e. one turnover, and I wasn't very aggressive when it came to taking open shots. It takes a slacker a while to warm up to new situations. Later that week, the coach called me in his office and told me that from what he had seen, I couldn't play varsity. He suggested I play Junior Varsity. A slacker play Junior Varsity, I don't think so! Now tell me this, how could I hurt a team that hadn't won a game in nearly two years? The whole school could be on Varsity and still do no worse. Well, I went to one practice of the Junior Varsity and decided, no, this isn't for me.

I later noticed that the coach had decided to work with a 6'9" slacker that had never played basketball before. Instead of working with the guys that were motivated, losers and all, he decided to spend more time on his unproven Miracle Boy. We had one student that was 4'9"; we called him "Johnny Red." Johnny Red would play the Slacker Miracle Boy at lunchtime one-on-one. He would run circles around him. The score was never even close. The Slacker Miracle Boy, eventually lost his desire, and quit half way through the season.

We ended up winning the second to the last game of the season, blowing our chances for the longest losing streak the state had ever seen.

The coach eventually quit teaching and his coaching job. I'm not sure where he ended up.

Rotten Floors and Corn Bread –

I had always wanted to go to the same schools that my Mom, Dad, and brothers had gone too. I was very excited that I would be able to attend the same junior high and high school that my family attended. Much to my dismay, they changed the school boundaries, so I had to attend a small country school close by. The first day I was there, a student was running in the gym when he was stopped abruptly. His leg had gone through a rotten part of the gym floor. Apparently no one knew about it and he was the one un-lucky enough to find it. He broke his leg.

That same day, the school cafeteria was serving corn bread. I was never a big fan of corn bread, and this little event wasn't going to change my mind. I put some butter on it to make it a little more palatable, corn bread can be so dry, and when I was about half way through, I noticed that something was scratching my throat. Little did I know I was jawing on a hair that was about seven inches long. I had already swallowed about half of it when I discovered the intruder. Have you ever had to pull a hair out of your esophagus? Believe me it's not pleasant.

I later noticed a slacker food server without a hair net. Why should she wear one? She wasn't eating, and even if she were, what's the big deal about eating your own hair.

Don't Blame Us -

One of our rivals in high school had a football team that hadn't won a game the whole season. They had been manhandled all year, and very rarely scored. When we played them, all I ever heard was, don't expect much, we haven't had a team very long. Well, that was true for the time being; but when they hadn't won a game during the second, third, fourth, and finally the fifth year, you realized you were dealing with a large number of loser slacker boys. It wasn't until the current batch of slackers had graduated and moved on, did they ever start to have a winning season.

Slacker attitudes can have a large effect on those around them. Slackerism breeds Slackerism, just as it bred the losers on this team. So if you are industrious, beware the slacker co-worker/student, you might end up using excuse after excuse for your failures.

The coach we had for football wasn't a slacker as much as he just had other priorities. He had a number of players that were rather good, so he just didn't try to develop his other players much.

I played a lot of football growing up. I grew up in the era of Dick Butkus and Gale Sayers. I loved the Chicago Bears. They were the greatest, even if they didn't always have a winning record. The 85 season was incredible. I was too young to notice the win in 63.

I always wanted to be Gale Sayers, cutting, slicing, and blowing by each opponent. With that dream, I decided to go out for football. I had never played organized ball before, so it was a little intimidating. I would try out at the beginning of each season. We would have two conditioning practices a day. It was mainly for physical conditioning to handle the hot Indiana sun. I was a running back, yet I never ran the ball in practice. This wasn't good. I remember being called upon to go out and run a Power I Right 24. It was in the "I" formation, and I would be running the ball just off the right guard up the middle. I only weighed 125 lbs. at that time so running up the middle was a little lame.

We were playing our archrivals that had never won a game. I figured coach thought it was no big deal if he gave me a chance. I got the ball, and ran the play exactly as designed, but there was no blocking, no front line. About four defenders hit me. I think I ran for maybe two yards.

One other time, coach sent me out for a kick-off return. I had never done this in practice either. The ball came my way; I picked it up and handed-off to our prime running back. Sure, that may have been the smartest thing to do, he was better than I was, but that was my big chance, my chance to shine and prove myself. I never got to run the ball again in a game, or in practice. I blew it.

In case you're wondering, I was a freshman at the time. I needed a little guidance and encouragement, just like so many other kids at that age. It's unfortunate for slackers to have regrets.

There's a Rat in the Dryer –

While I was in college, I worked for my parents in their appliance store. I handled sales and service. I remember one time, a couple had called me to come and look at their clothes dryer. The tub wouldn't turn, nor would the dryer run. I arrived at their home and started to check things out. Sure enough, it wouldn't run. It was shutting off on its motor overload. I tried to turn the drum by hand and it wouldn't budge. I took the front of the dryer off and tried to turn the shaft of the motor by hand to no avail. I attached a set of vice-grips on the shaft, and still had no luck, it still wouldn't move. I thought the motor had seized. I had one last slacker thought of brilliance; I looked at the back of the dryer and pulled off the vent pipe. I noticed there was no outside flap on the exhaust leading outside. That's not good; critters can come in that way. I reached my hand into the exhaust of the dryer and felt something furry. I immediately pulled it out, and quickly. The Hanta virus was big in the news at that time, and if you know anything about it; it's deadly. Yellowstone Park is having issues with this too. At the time, eighty percent of those that contracted it died, your lungs fill up so quickly with fluid you literally drown. There was very little they could do about it.

Either way, it was up to me to remedy the problem. I looked around for something to use to pull the critter out. I found a pair of women's panties that had fallen behind the dryer and covered my hand with them. I slipped my hand into the back of the dryer slowly hoping all the time that whatever it was was dead. Sure enough, it was dead. It was about an eight-inch long rat, skinny tail and all. It had made contact with the 220 V terminals and been electrocuted. I yelled out, "It's a dead rat!" The woman of the house was very embarrassed of course. You knew this was coming, if they hadn't been raised slackers, they would have had a flap on that exhaust, and no rats would have gotten in.

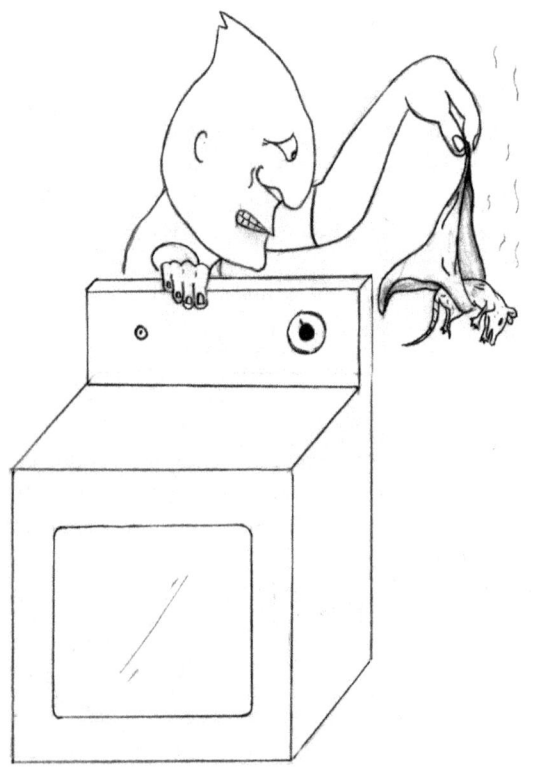

Eighth Grade Track –

I loved to run when I was in the eighth-grade. The more I could run the better. Our PE teacher was also our track coach. To coin a phrase, "killing two birds with one stone" he would have us run track during PE. I would practice very hard. I hoped that it would improve my speed and increase my endurance. I ran the "440" and mile relay on the track team. During one PE period, I was running myself to death as usual, but didn't have a clue as to what was coming my way. One student, Slacker Todd, never ran much faster than a slow jog during PE practice. He just wasn't going to exert the energy. He was saving himself for a more opportune time, and opportune time it was. Our coach wanted us to have a race to see who was going to run in the upcoming conference championships. I was on the starting team, believe it or not, and Todd wasn't involved in either the "440" or mile relay. I think he ran the "880." Coach wanted to determine if Todd should also be involved in my two events. We lined up to race. I was already very tired from practicing so hard, and conversely, Todd was ready to rock-and-roll. The coach allowed others to run alongside of us during the heat. This didn't make it any easier; they were clogging up the lanes. Todd beat me, and by a long margin. I was then told I would be an alternate for the conference. I would be allowed to ride the bus and watch the events from the sidelines. Sorry, I am not the type to sit the bench, or watch from the sidelines for anyone. It doesn't do me or anyone else any good to be a spectator. Yes I know, that's not exhibiting teamwork, but there certainly isn't any "teamwork" for me or others to be watching from the stands. If you did or still do sit the bench, more power to you, not me. If I'm to add any benefit, I must play at some point or another. If not, what possible good can I do? I didn't go, nor did I ever run competitively again. There's a pattern forming here isn't there? Wow, this is sad. If the coach had warned me about the race, would I have conserved my energy and beat Todd, perhaps?

Please tell me what ever happened to loyalty and rewarding those who work the hardest? Well, you and I both know the answer to that. Winning is everything even in Jr. High track.

Anger and the Low Rider –

While working at a production facility, a man had come up to me early one morning and asked when the production workers went on break. I wasn't really thinking, as slackers never do, so I told him. At break-time his girlfriend came out for a smoke with the "Herd" where he then proceeded to beat her to a pulp. Three other production workers jumped him and prevented him from doing any further harm to her.

Someone called our campus security. They arrived about ten minutes later. They had no way to subdue him. No rope, handcuffs, or zip-ties. They called the county sheriff to come and take care of the matter. In the meantime, the gutless slacker decides to make a run for it. He takes off running around the side of one of our buildings with the security guard fast behind him and another employee running around the opposite side of the building to head him off. The great thing was that he was wearing his pants according to the new "low rider" style. They were barely hanging on the back of his bottom. You've seen them, boxers showing and all. He barely made 15 yards before his pants fell down around his ankles. He tripped, thus allowing the security guard to catch up and apprehend him.

The guy wasn't man enough to talk over his problems with his girlfriend, so he decided to be a "real man" and beat her. Of course a real slacker doesn't wear his pants down to his knees either. He skinned his knee during the fall and drew some blood. We were all afraid that he would turn around and sue the company. Now that would be American justice.

Bathroom Slackers –

The same production facility, in which I worked, had many slackers that didn't seem to know how to use a urinal. On many occasions, there would be urine underneath the urinal, instead of where it belonged, and they would never flush. I always wanted to make a sign that said, "If you do not know how to flush the urinal, ask and training will be provided." Although I don't know who would have performed the training, not me!

At my new company, a number of slackers would clean their coffee cups in the bathroom and then leave them on the vanity beside the faucets. The last time this happened, they left them there for almost seven weeks. I finally moved them and placed them underneath the sink. Another week passed and they were still there. When they were on the vanity, soap and water would runoff from your hands as you washed them and splash into the cups. The vanity was very small. Finally, I decided to have some fun. I moved the cups and placed them underneath the urinal. I made a sign that said,

"ETS Challenge"
- Hit the urinal, five points,
- Hit any cup, ten points,
- Fill a cup, twenty points.

Needless to say, some co-workers found this very funny, while the culprits didn't. Someone ripped my sign off the wall and crumpled it up into a little bitty ball. They then picked up the cups and placed them back on the vanity. Some slacker, I do not know who, removed three of the cups, and placed two of them under the toilet in the stall. As far as I know, they are still there to this day. Who knows what happened to the third?

Road Construction Slackers –

I know we have all experienced this; but never the less, this is my story. Every spring in Indiana we have a particular flower that pops up all over our highways; the "orange-blossom cone." The cone restricts highway movement by narrowing down parts of the road to generally one lane. Neither Ortho weed spray, Weed-B-Gone nor ChemLawn were capable of removing or killing these cones. The cones would go up long before slacking (construction) began, and stay up long after the construction slackers had left.

On many, many occasions, the "site" was set for construction to begin, but no construction workers would show for weeks. I guess they just wanted to warn everyone that "work" might be starting soon. Finally, when they did begin their work, you would see, for instance, one guy filling in a pot hole, painting a line, or directing other slackers, while two or three others were drinking their "big slurpy" and just slacking away. This really sounds like a commercial. Maybe it sounds like the TSA at JFK?

The most frustrating thing was the traffic jams that would occur because of the one lane. The construction slackers didn't seem to care how much of a problem their "lack of work" caused others. I tell ya, slacking, basking in the sun with your buddies, along with a Big Slurpy, what a job, what a job.

During the "construction season/event," many drivers would be well aware that the road was narrowing down to one lane, yet they wouldn't get in the proper lane until the last minute. Quite often, this would create an even bigger traffic jam, because others wouldn't let them in. They would both jockey for position and fight each other for the ever-narrowing space. Slackers aren't very polite, even to other slackers.

Cubes –

Do you work in a cube at your business? I do. Bub asked my opinion on some things one day, and being the slacker I am I asked him what answer he was looking for. He said an honest answer. Can you get an honest answer from a slacker?

He was also working on our department's budget, so I asked him if I could have a roof put on my cube, maybe a thatch roof as seen on the huts in Gilligan's Island. Some of those 1970's door beads would be nice too. I told him that a cot to put under my desk for napping, and a small refrigerator for drinks and snacks would also be great. He said it all sounded like an episode of Seinfeld. I said sure it does, perhaps Seinfeld stole my idea in the first place.

I supervised some 12 temporaries for about 15 months in one job. They were such a delight. Some were very good and dedicated, and others had a work ethic that left a lot to be desired.

They were the epitome of worker-bee slackers. They would come in late, or not come in at all. Some would come in and develop "boredom illness" and go home early. Others would "pad" their time cards. Still others would just get bored with what they were doing and then start to create some excitement/trouble with other co-workers. For instance, about every two weeks or so, there would be a "blow-up." One worker would let some petty thing that another had said get to him. They would then be at each other's throats shouting obscenities, and various other put-downs. I would then have to get involved, make a few threats, and implore them to act like civilized human beings, with the hope that they would settle down for a while. They would, only until next time.

One time we were planning on having a department cookout in the local park. Everyone had signed up to bring something or another. One worker was to bring the lighter fluid and charcoal. Another worker had made the statement, that if Slacker Sara didn't bring "Kingsford" charcoal; it probably wouldn't light very well. Another worker, who over-heard this statement, went to Slacker Sara and told her about it. Slacker Sara was irate. So on the day of the cookout, Sara told us we would not be allowed to use her lighter fluid or charcoal. Now picture this, we had hamburgers, hot-dogs, and all the fixins, but no way to cook them.

I tried to reason with Slacker Sara, but to no avail. We had to go buy additional fluid and charcoal to have the cookout. Slacker Sara continued to be outraged. She started blaming the other worker for her own behavior. This was classic displacement tactics. She said she didn't care about the job, so that was a surprise, and that she didn't care if we fired her. Well, the temp agency did fire her (but not because she wouldn't let us use her charcoal). Be careful for what you wish for, it might just come true. What's that about "looking before you leap"?

Decomposed ? –

I went to a slacker's house one day to look at their faulty gas range. A client had called and told me they needed some work done. I knocked on the door to find three drunken women and two of their drunken cohorts. It wasn't the most inviting atmosphere, their appearance, their breath!

I had a responsibility to try and repair the range. The gas oven wouldn't light. I checked the control, the burner, the pilot light, and the valve. The harassment came when I bent over to look at the burner in the oven. The three slacking women started telling me what they would like to do to me sexually. Their slacker boyfriends were not amused. Slackers should really be devoted to one man or woman at a time. It really isn't too cool to come-on to another slacker in front of your significant other. Their slacker boy friends were looking at me as if they would just as soon see me dead. I tried to get their women off me as the subject. Let's talk about the weather; let's talk about the soap opera you're watching, anything but me!

In the meantime, I decided to find the shut-off valve to the range. There was none found behind the range, so I decided it must be down in the basement. At this point I was not treasuring the prospect of being raped by three drunken women, and then murdered by their slacking men. I went down to the basement, getting more nervous and frustrated at the same time. There was no light down there. I was trying to find the shut-off valve by the light of a small basement window. While looking, I found I kept sticking to the floor. I would lift one foot only to find the other sticking to something else. I called up stairs for them to bring me a flashlight. When they did, they shined the light down at my feet to find that I was stuck to the insides of a dead cat! Apparently, the cat had crawled through the small open window and couldn't find its way back out. I wasn't very happy at this point. I told them it was the valve on their range, and that it was too old to fix. I scraped the remains of the cat off of my shoes on the edge of the basement steps as I left.

You know, even slackers should keep their house clean. Is this your house? No dead cats please.

Gross and Grosser Yet –

My father had one rental where he had originally rented to a family of seven. They stopped paying their rent after a couple of months. He asked them what was going on and tried to work with them for an additional few months, but that didn't help. He eventually had to execute an eviction order. That took another 30 days to get the slackers out of the house. By the time they did leave, 21 people were living there. In the meantime, their utilities had been shut off for lack of payment. It was right in the middle of an Indiana summer, hot and humid. No gas, no electricity, no running water, steamy even.

My Dad informed me one morning that he had a job for me. He handed me a broom, a bucket, and a shovel. Do you know where this is leading, I didn't. When I arrived, I was grossed out to find a refrigerator full of rotting food, and the place full of roaches. That wasn't the worst of it; I went into the downstairs bathroom to check it out. What I found was incredibly sick. Not only had they continued to use the toilet, when they filled it up with human debri, they then proceeded to fill the bathtub. I now understood what I was to use the shovel and bucket for. I was to shovel out the toilet and bathtub until they were clean. What a disturbing disgusting job. I did the shoveling, slackers can shovel with the best of them, but I didn't do any additional cleaning. I told my Dad that he could fire me if he liked, but that I was done! Slackers should have some standards, even if they are low.

The Babel apartments had called me to take a look at one of their refrigerators that wasn't working properly. The woman at the apartment had a very bitter disposition. Yes, even more than mine. I started to check out the system, when she struck up conservation with me. She asked me where my Dad worked. I told her he worked in the Display Advertising Department with the local newspaper. She said, "Well that's not anything to brag about is it?" I said, it's surely better than most and that my Dad seemed to like it okay. She then started talking about God, Heaven, and Hell. She said, "I suppose you believe in Heaven?" I said I did. She said, "That's a bunch of @#$%." I tried to testify to her about what Heaven was all about, and that life was really worth living. She told me "We are all like a bunch of worms, here today and dead tomorrow." What a shame, even slackers know better than that. I told her we were created in the image of God. This didn't change her disposition. She continued to hammer me. I really wanted to just fix the refrigerator and leave. I finally said, "you are just about the meanest old woman I have ever met, with the attitude you have, no wonder you're so bitter." That probably wasn't the best thing to say to her. She did quiet down. Perhaps she thought about what I said. I don't know. I hope so. I'm really sorry I didn't handle that better. I repaired the refrigerator and left shortly thereafter.

Now there's nothing worse than a slacker that would rip another slacker off. Slackers out there, you know very well that there will be plenty of others who will rip you off from time-to-time, but to do it to another slacker just goes against the Slacker Convention. The Slacker Convention has been around for a long time. Most modern nations have adopted the standards, and most abide by it. Take France and most of the European nations for instance; sub-40 hour workweek, 5 to 6 weeks' worth of vacation mandated by law, wow, I need to move. Wait, no I don't, we will soon be with them, and sooner than we think. Trillion's in debt, no economic growth, excessive regulatory standards that stunt growth and ingenuity, great.

Please order your own copy of the Articles of Slackerism from the USA (United Slackers of America) Institute. Read it. Study it. Live it. If they had a web site, the address would be www.UnitedSlackersofAmerica.sla.

Believe me, I have run across my own share of deadbeat slackers, and it isn't pleasant. I was working on a slacker's refrigerator for my parents business; the refrigerator would no longer keep things cool. In fact, it wouldn't even run. Its relay, the device that momentarily kicks in to start the compressor, was bad. I replaced it and it started working properly.

About a week later, the slacker calls me back. His refrigerator had stopped working again. I went back and found that the system's cooling lines had a restriction in them. This would be a physical blockage caused by a bad refrigerant (Freon) filter, or frozen particles. Either way it will prevent "Freon" from flowing, and thus no cooling. Don't even get me started on "Freon," Al Gore, and the new religion of global warming. Oh I'm sorry, it's Climate Change now. Call it whatever to keep that research money coming in. We forget the fact that our climate changes on a daily basis and has for centuries, even before man ever stepped foot on this planet. I digress once again. I informed him of the problem and that it would require some major surgery to repair. It also had absolutely nothing to do with the first problem. Being a "rip-off slacker", and being rather "slow," he didn't see it that way. He proceeded to cuss me out and refused to pay me for the second call.

Slackers, please learn to control your tongue. Just because you're a slacker, educated or not, you can still show some integrity and restraint and not use foul language.

When you're angry with someone, instead of cussing them out you could act like the Three Stooges. You could poke them in the eye, hit them on the head, put your fingers up to your ears, wiggle them, stick out your tongue, and make faces, but don't swear. Slackers should also not get smart with other non-slackers. My father-in-law always says, "Don't get smart with me, it's not like ya!"

When I went on another appliance repair call, the slacker's had a problem with their electric hot water heater. Both elements were okay, from an electrical standpoint, but both were also totally corroded from lime deposits. They were on a well, and the lime had done its job over the years. The elements would no longer transmit heat adequately to the water passing over them. They needed replaced. I informed the slackers that it would cost them around $90 to repair. The slacker homemaker said she needed to talk it over with her husband. She sent me on my way without payment.

I called them back about a week later and asked them if they still wanted me to repair their water heater. The slack-husband got on the phone and stated that he had gotten another opinion and that "I had screwed him over." In addition, I "didn't even know how to use a

Volt-Ohm-Meter." I asked him what the other firm had done and how much they charged him he said "they had replaced the entire water heater, and that it cost him $300.00." Now what did he say, "I had screwed him over?" I could have made the repairs for $90. My math may not be that good, but I believe that's a savings of $210.00. Even for a slacker, that should mean something.

Slacker Arson Inspector -

Something that is crucial is that slackers have no business being in positions of importance, i.e. CEO's, CFO's, running Freddie Mac and Fannie May, the Federal government, managers, supervisors, policemen, doctors, nurses, medical technologists, teachers, and yes, arson inspectors.

My parents had one gentleman that had served in WWII. He was a decorated veteran. He had a Purple Heart from the war. He also had a drinking and smoking problem. His problem was so bad that he had lost his wife and kids, as well as his job. When he wasn't drinking he was fun to be around and was just a great guy. When he was drinking, he was miserable. He was very self-centered, whiny, mean, and cried a lot.

He had gotten involved with a woman that didn't have the greatest reputation. She had tried to black-male him into making payments to her to keep her mouth shut about a supposed baby she was carrying. It wasn't his. He refused, yet she continued to make threats and continued to harass him over a number of months. This didn't help his emotional state. He drank and drank some more. Some of his binges would last weeks.

My parents had recently replaced the dead bolt lock on his apartment door. He had requested we do so because he thought the woman had a spare key. About a week later, my father received a phone call that one of his apartments was on fire. My father arrived to find that the man had been burned beyond recognition. He looked like a burnt marshmallow. I was then assigned to clean out the apartment and get it ready to rent to a new tenant. We called his relatives to come and get his personal belongings, but they never came.

I started the clean up the next Monday morning, but I noticed some things that were rather peculiar. For instance, I found canceled checks that had been written to the woman and they were not in the gentleman's hand writing, the key that matched the old dead bolt had been jammed in the key hole of the new lock, and been broken off. There was no way to open the door except by using the deadbolt. The only reason it was open now was because the fire department had kicked it in. There was a half empty gas can in the back parking lot, and the fire had been so intense, that it melted his TV, and a dish washing liquid bottle located in the kitchen of the next room. Yet, the sofa where the gentleman had died had burnt down to the floor only where his legs had been located.

Now, I'm no arson inspector, but if he were drunk, and been smoking at the same time, why wouldn't the part of the sofa where his torso been located, have burnt the worst? I called the Fire Department. They sent out an inspector, and I told him of my findings, and I didn't even have a trained eye. He blew it off. The gentlemen's relatives didn't care, so no one else did. The fire department said it was a smoking related accident. Wow, isn't that convenient.

Please don't put slackers in positions of importance, i.e. CEO's, CFO's, running Freddie Mac and Fannie May, the Federal government, managers, supervisors, policemen, doctors, nurses, medical technologists, teachers, and most of all, arson inspectors.

I was in fourth grade when I got my first experience at being abused by an angry teacher.

A couple of other students had been throwing spitballs at me. They were the kind of little pieces of paper that you roll up tightly, put in your mouth to get wet so they throw better, and then bomb away. Sometimes we would shoot them through straws like a blowpipe. Meg and Bandy ganged up on me one day during class. I was bombarded. They were all over my desk and all over the floor. I retaliated of course, but I wasn't very sneaky about it. I think they were keeping watch for each other, because when I sent my salvo over, I was nailed. Mrs. D. came over and asked me if I threw those spitballs? I said yes, and that Greg and Sandy had too. She walloped the side of my face with the palm of her hand. It hurt! I was in one of those old time wooden desks with the metal frame. The kind of desk where the top hinged up to get to your books, and the chair swiveled to allow you to get in and out easier. The blow spun me partially around in my seat. I swiveled back around to face her, with the entire class now watching intensely, and she asked again, did you throw those spit balls, I said yes, and that Greg and Sandy did too. She smacked me again, just as hard as the first time. I spun back around again, and she asked once again, did you throw those spit balls, and this time, with my face smarting on both sides, I just said yes. She was happy with that.

Mrs. D. wasn't very interested in the truth; she was only interested in what she had seen, me throwing the spitballs. You will find that slackers aren't very interested in the truth. They also don't like tattle-tails. Beware of what you say, it just might come back to smack you!

The Oak Pointer Stick and Mrs. G.

I was in second grade, and at that time in history, my school was teaching "See-and-Say," no phonics, just memorization of a certain number of words. Our favorite book was "Fun with Dick and Jane." You remember, see Dick run. See Jane run after Dick. See Spot catch the ball. See Spot spot the fire hydrant.

I remember a number of my best friends not catching on to the "See-and-Say" very well. They needed phonics, as all of us did and still do. They just couldn't memorize as well as the rest of us. I was doing okay. We had a kind of early-term placement test to see where we belonged, in "See-and Say" or in the Phonics class. I decided I wanted to be with my friends so I "threw" the test and flunked.

I was now in the phonics class with my buddies. Life was great, but we had Mrs. G for a teacher. She always had one of those oak paddles with holes drilled in it to keep us in fear, and in line. She also had an oak pointer stick for pointing out things on the chalkboard. One of my friends, named Steve, was laughing about something one day. Mrs. G. mistook me for Steve and promptly, and very hard I might add, cracked me over the top of the head with her pointer stick. It hurt. In fact she not only cracked me over the head, she cracked the stick as well. She was so upset at damaging the stick; she had to get a new one. She wasn't the least bit upset at the knot on my head. It must have taken hours for the swelling to go down.

You must be thinking where on earth did you go to school? I went to a small country school in the middle of an Indiana cornfield. We were well disciplined. Most people back then didn't think a thing about some of the stuff we sue over today. In fact, if the parents of the Littleton, CO losers had an oak pointer stick, then maybe their little angels wouldn't have gone off the deep end and resorted to killing innocent kids. Let's not even talk about Virginia Tech, or Arizona and the Congresswoman.

Dr. VA –

We had one slacker professor in college that recorded all of his lectures on tape. He then required you to go to the "Chem. Lab" to listen to them. Have you ever tried to listen to a professor for an entire hour on tape, especially one that taught analytical chemistry? It's incredibly boring, but listen we did. If you had any questions, he would have a one-hour question and answer session once a week. It wasn't very helpful.

By using the slacker tape method, he never had to present a formal lecture ever. He could stay in his office all day, play computer games, and never be bothered by students. Now that is Slacker Utopia!

Degree Bigots –

Have you ever run across a "degree bigot?" A degree bigot is someone that discriminates against you because, 1) you have a degree that is different than theirs 2) you have a degree and they don't, or 3) you didn't go to the same school where they attended. It comes down to fear, arrogance, or jealousy. Fear that you will look better than they will, arrogance that they are better than you, or jealousy because you have what they don't.

My brother-in-law has a Mechanical Engineering Technology degree from Purdue University. In Indiana, you are only "allowed" to go to two schools, Indiana or Purdue. All of the other schools are considered, at least by a number of graduates from IU and Purdue, as less than a degree. I think they consider all other degrees as having a certificate from a vocational school. Not that there is anything wrong with vocational school. Anyway, my brother-in-law had gone to the "right" school, but he had a boss that wanted to discriminate against him anyway. He told him that he had the wrong engineering degree, even though his degree matched with what he was currently doing. See, to a slacker boss, what you have done in life, schooling, experience, etc., really doesn't matter; they will find anything to discriminate against you, and it doesn't matter what color you are.

Degree Bigots fail to realize we all have the capacity to learn and apply previous knowledge. Bottom line, they are petty and just don't seem to care.

Good luck dealing with these kinds of slackers. You really don't have a chance. Once you're pegged, it's over. If you do try to turn them around, you are greeted with arrogance and anger. The Bible says, "Speak not into the ears of a fool for they will hate you for the wisdom of your words." Proverbs 23:9

The Brown Toothbrush –

A friend of mine came home one day to visit. He had moved away to Seymour, IN where he had started his own insurance business and would occasionally come back home to Anderson for a visit. He was about to go out on a date and found that he had forgotten his toothbrush. He looked around the bathroom to see if he could find either a new one, or one that no one was using. I'm not sure about the one "no one was using." Anyway, he looked under the counter and found one in an old rusty can. That should have told him something. He started brushing his teeth and didn't notice that the brushes had been stained brown. I entered the bathroom to talk to him and started wondering where he had gotten the brush. I certainly didn't want him using mine. I said, "Dan, where did you get that brush?" He said, "What do you mean?" I replied, "Where did you get that brush?" He said, "Underneath the sink in that can." I said, "Dan, my Pro-Keds were dirty the other day. I had stepped in some dog poop and needed something to clean them with. The brush is for that purpose, cleaning things." He told me I was lying. I said, "Dan I'm not lying." "Did you not notice that the brush's bristles are stained brown?" At that point, he started spitting and frantically searching for some Scope or better yet, Listerine. He rinsed his mouth repeatedly with Listerine and didn't worry about finding another brush at home. I think he bought a new one before he came back that evening.

To this day, he has never used anything but his own toothbrush. Let this be a lesson to all slackers out there, brown bristles on a toothbrush is a telling sign.

Chapter 5: Slacker Fun Stuff

So on a lighter note; you're probably asking yourself, how can I be a better slacker at home and work? Allow me to provide you with some concrete examples and ideas. Perhaps you will be able to improve on these, and please do so while at work.

Lunchtime –

Always take at least 15 minutes longer than allowed. No one will really notice, and even if they did, hey what's 15 minutes?

Naps –

At one company I worked for, we call napping at work "doing the Ted." Ted was a guy that napped a lot during work hours.

You should always find an isolated place to nap. You can nap early in the morning, or just after lunch. If you are in a cube, or if in a lab, find a corner and face away from those you slack with. Number one; always have something in front of you that looks like work. You might have a Motor Trend, or another "gear head" magazine in the middle of some official looking documents. Just be prepared to close them when someone walks by. Always keep your ears open to the fact that someone might walk up and ask you to actually do some work.

If possible, learn how to sleep with your eyes open. A co-slacker of mine, at one firm, learned how to do this and was very good at it. He eventually became known as Bob "Slacker" McNed. We also had "King of Slacker West" Jack Mere, (This one knew how to get the free lunches and boondoggles better than anyone did), and we had a Slack Master Sharon McBeth.

If possible, keep company documents in front of you. When someone does walk by, awaken and turn a page every so often. It gives the impression you are working, even though you're not. Isn't it true that your brain is working even while you're sleeping, controlling non-voluntary muscles and other bodily functions, digestion, gas production, etc.?

One temporary worker, who had been with the company for over five years, temporary huh, had once stated, "ask not what you can do for your company, but what your company can do for you." He was a natural born slacker. We tip our hats to you, Master Slacker, Chief Milker and Gravy Boat Skipper, Slacker Tom McMillan. Tom created a photo album once for another slacker before he left the company. Of course he did it on company time, and after hours, that way he was paid time and a half.

Speaking of Gravy Boats, let's ponder for a moment. Can you imagine actually cruising on a "Gravy Boat?" The seas are nothing but pure gravy with smooth sailing all the way. There you are in the Master's quarters setting in your body contoured heated leather Lazy Boy, watching the 1998 NBA Eastern Conference finals. It's the Bulls vs. the Pacers once again, except this time the Pacers win! Okay, it's the 1999 NBA Eastern Conference finals. It's the Knicks vs. the Pacers once again, except this time the Pacers win! It may be the NBA finals where it's the Lakers vs. Pacers and the Pacers win!

I'm still waiting for the Pacers to get back to the finals. This past season was good when playing the Heat. The Heat took a page out of Reggie Miller's playbook when instituting the "Heat Flop." That's when you are barely touched by an opposing player you flop back and then fall to the floor. The NBA refs take note, and if you are a big name like James or Wade, you generally get the call to go your way. The disparity between the calls was amazing. It wasn't the year for the Pacers. The Heat were ordained when James arrived. The Pacers have trouble just making the playoffs, whether self-inflicted or with the help of the NBA, it's just hard to get there.

Now back to our book. Your chair has a built in refrigerator and bathroom, so you don't have to expand any unnecessary energy. You have slacker wenches waiting on you hand and foot; or for you slacker ladies out there, slacker wench-mates. You cruise to the Bahamas, Tahiti, Cancun, and Hawaii; all while your Gravy Boat Captain, Slacker Tom McMillan, has the ship set on cruise control so he can enjoy slacking as well. This is indeed Slacker Paradise. You'll come home with one of the best slacker tans you have ever had. If you don't like slacker Gravy Boats, than you could always ride the Gravy Train through the Rockies and beyond!

Company Sponsored Events –

We had a hot-dog lunch one day, and the flyer stated that the lunch would be from 11 until 2. A true slacker interprets this to mean, take lunch from 11 until 2, all 3 hours. That's what the flyer said.

In order not to get "caught" doing what the flyer said, you can slack in your car, slack at the location where the lunch took place, the obvious is sometimes the best cover, slack in the bathroom, and slack in different buildings where others on campus work.

Company Internet Access –

Always, always, always, cover your tracks. When you are accessing job web pages to apply for better slacker positions, always erase the "History" "Cookies" and "Internet Temporary Files." Sure there are other ways to track your "inquiries" but why give your "superiors" any more firepower than you have to. You can always say you were looking for a job for your slacker brother-in-law. Once again, remember to have an answer ready to cover your tracks. Plausible denial is the name of the game. The sad thing today is Big Brother is watching in so many ways, from the many MIS tools available, to keystroke trackers, it's really hard now for a slacker to stay under the radar, so you must be very careful. Sooner or later they will deploy small non-military predator drones to spy on us, now that will be interesting.

Sick Days –

Make sure you know what the company policy is for sick days. Determine how many you can take per month/year and decide how to spread them out. Don't spread them out evenly, and always take the full amount. After all, slacking requires you be well rested. It is truly an acting job after all. Remember the slacker managers? Learn from the best. They didn't move up the corporate ladder because they were competent. I know that's not nice.

When calling in "sick," always do it first thing in the morning. Your voice will be at its worst then. You'll sound your sickest. Find out what's been going around, and before you call in, pretend you've have been coming down with something at least 2-3 days before. That way, it won't be a surprise when you do call.

Thanks to modern technology you can call in and leave your message on your boss's voice mail. That way you don't have to personally talk to him/her and be "grilled" about why you're sick. Disconnect your phone or shut off you cell, some managers will not be deterred by your message and will call to find out what's going on. You just told them via voice mail, they don't need any more information than that. Better yet, send a text and then shut your phone off.

Playing Games on Your Computer at Work

Most MIS departments have taken all the joy out of playing games on your PC or Laptop. The games are simply not allowed to be loaded. Anyway, if you still do have access to games, always have a "hot button" that takes you to a spreadsheet or Word document that you have been working on. Someone might come in and not understand. Just be sure you have saved it sometime during the day so it looks like it's been updated. It's not good to have a document that is six months old and a date to prove it. If push comes to shove, tell them you were going through old files to delete. Concerning the game, tell them the game had been up there since lunch and you were just about to close it out.

If you can get Administrative privileges you can then load whatever you want on your computer. Just be aware that they will be monitoring you remotely and you really don't want that kind of grief coming your way. All slackers are asking is "Give peace a chance." If I'm not bothering you, then don't bother me. Live and let live, very Libertarian.

Bathroom Breaks –

The bathroom is a very good place to slack. No one really knows how long you have been in the stall, and probably won't ask. It can sometimes take up to 20 minutes or longer to "go" especially if you're having a difficult time. Even if you're not, you can always use this as an excuse.

Bring three to four pair of shoes to work. Keep them out of view, and change them throughout the day. This way when you are taking a bathroom slacker break, the type of shoes you are wearing won't easily identify you when someone looks under the bathroom stall. I hear Bruno Mollies are nice.

In order to make your bathroom break more pleasurable, take a nap, or place a magazine down the front of your shirt before entering the stall, and then just read for a while. Always have a technical journal with you. You want to make it look like you're really working when coming out of the stall.

Old Beat-up Car –

Slackers always drive around in old beat-up cars. Even if it's in good shape, it should look as if it's about to break down. Bald tires, loud exhaust, perhaps dragging the ground, give the definite impression your car breaks down, and often. Slackers use this to their advantage. Your boss knows how much you make and that you can't possibly afford a new car, so why not have it "break down" about 3 to 4 times a year; when it's finally "up and running" come in around 10 or 11 am, so what if you're supposed to be there by 8. This way you can sleep-in and have additional rest time throughout the year.

Bereavement –

This is an excellent way to skip work. Just make sure you know the company policy and how many days you get. Remember that your parents can only die once, unless you have stepparents. If you change bosses frequently, or change companies often, you can use this excuse more than once. The bereavement flowers you receive from your company always add a nice touch and certain flare when slacking, I mean, bereaving at home.

Reading Glasses –

When working, it's always nice to have an "eye ailment" this way you can wear dark glasses and nap at the same time. It's also good to wear glasses with safety side-shields; that way no one can see your eyes from an angle when you're snoozing.

Campus Cruising –

Strolls around the complex - Always have a clipboard with you to make it look like you're fast at work collecting data. Maybe even have a Fed Ex package in hand to look as if you're about to send something important out.

Pawning –

Now let's talk about pawning your work on others. Perhaps you're on a project that you happen to like. Is there a way to stretch it out so you don't have to do something "less desirable"? Then do it. Can you go to your boss and whine "that your plate is just too full?" Then do it. Are there ways you can present some co-worker as more qualified to do the really lousy stuff? Then do it. Is there an opportunity to steal someone's idea and then present it at an important meeting, thus making you look suddenly more competent? Then do it. Is there an opportunity to not work at all and attend as many meetings as possible? Then do it!

Get involved in as many projects and employee teams you can. Get your boss to agree that you are the departments best slacker, and perhaps you will never have to work again. You will be given kudos for caring, and "busting your rear," all the while adding absolutely no value to the company. Remember Slacker Bub? Your position and pay will balloon. You will able to add new multiple skills to your resume. Companies love to see that you have done so many different and worthless things. Remember to build your resume with all of the key words and phrases, none that have any real meaning of course.

Company Trips –

Always convince your boss that an extra week's work is needed when away on business, even though perhaps only one day will suffice. How much can you spend per meal? Find out and spend it! How much "entertaining" can you do? Find out and do it! Is it possible to bring your spouse or children? Then do it!

If your company has already scheduled you to attend a seminar or big "fat cat" meeting that has to be rescheduled, then why not try to see if you can "stall the process of cancellation." That way, by the time they find out it will be too late. You might as well go because there is no sense in wasting all that time, money, and effort.

Take your clues from your slacker bosses. Is there a way you can attend an industry show? You know very well that shows are all about boondoggles. So go for it. A week off from work, and family, all paid for by the company, what slacker could ask for more? Hanging out by the pool isn't bad either.

Company Lunches –

Always make sure you talk about something related to work, even if it's the new wallpaper design in the bathroom. That way you can put the lunch on your corporate American Express. For instance, we were talking about Japanese culture the other day and related it to American culture and the corporate culture at my firm. This allowed us to have lunch on the company.

If your department or another department is taking someone out for their last day at work, is there a way you can say you worked with him even if you didn't? If there is, then you just got yourself a free lunch. Cool!

IT/MIS/IM - Support –

Have you ever been at work and decided you really didn't like what you had to do on your computer? Well, is there a way to get MIS (Management Information Systems) involved? MIS can be wonderful partners in the slacking business. For instance, do you need to upgrade your Windows application from 95A, 95B, 3.1, 98, XP, Vista, Windows 07/08 or any number of the latest MS upgrades? MIS informed me that this would require the removal of my computer for an entire day. If you know them well enough, perhaps you can bribe them to have additional "technical difficulties" so it takes them 2 days instead of one. Since so much today is done by PC/Laptop, how could you even be remotely productive without one?

Ponder –

Some slackers find that they need to "ponder." Pondering is about analyzing a situation, discussing issues with yourself, or just thinking about what your next slacker move will be. For example, I saw a slacker the other day printing out the entire Help files to Word, Excel, PowerPoint, Access, and Outlook. What an excellent way to slack. You give the impression that you're working diligently on your PC and printing out information, all the while using company resources, wasting time and just pondering away the hours.

Campus Smokers –

Some of the best slackers I have observed are smokers. If you don't smoke, maybe you should think about taking it up. Smokers take breaks about every hour or so. Think about it, you could average anywhere from 7 to 9 extra breaks a day. At an average of 5 to 7 minutes a break, this would constitute nearly 16,380 minutes of extra slack time per year. How else can you take an additional 5.25 hours per week, or 273 hours per year? You know that's almost an extra 7 weeks of slacking a year. When you eventually develop a smoking related illness, you can use your company's health plan for treatment; and utilize additional sick days. If you can prove that your illness was caused from smoking at work, you could sue your employer for allowing you to smoke there in the first place. This is definite a win/win situation. I see hundreds of thousands of dollars in your future.

The best smokers never empty their car ashtrays into a "proper" container. They always throw their "butts" out the widow while driving, or at an intersection. The best of the best just dump their ashtrays in a store parking lot. Well, they really don't respect themselves, so why should they respect the environment.

Please help me understand something, if you smoke, and enjoy it like you say, why do you drive with your driver's side window cracked? If you enjoy smoking so much, then why not keep the windows closed and enjoy all of the smoke. Why let any of it escape? I'm just asking.

Back Problems –

Many slackers develop back problems at an early age. Mowing, taking out the trash, lifting your little sister to change her diaper, are now all out of the question. Once you become an adult, you will have developed a long track record of back problems, and this will have allowed you to get out of so many undesirable situations.

Remember, you may not want to develop back problems until you have obtained a slacker position with a company that provides a good health plan. You could rely on "Obamacare" but we really don't know how that is going to work out, do we? Don't forget long-term disability. If anything, your back problem should be due to a company related accident. Make sure you check up on all your wonderful government disability benefits. Were in debt at a tune of >16 Trillion, what's a few extra Trillion here and there? Can anyone say "EBT" card?

Half Days –

I noticed a co-slacker had taken off a morning last week. She came in at 11:30 and then promptly took lunch. This is just great. To take off the whole morning and then go immediately to lunch is just too good. This is the type of slacking mind-set that all of us need to develop.

Internal Company Lunches –

If possible, get with the administrative assistant in your building and find out the schedule for lunches. Cookies and fruit plate meetings are my favorite. Whether you're invited or not, if you can get there before the meeting starts, take an extra plate and prepare to chow down back at your desk.

The caterers generally deliver the goods some fifteen minutes before each meeting is to occur. If you show up right before, the food is there for the taking. If you can't make it in time, then try to be there right after so you can be the first "vulture" to take care of the remains. So what if you take up additional work time to "determine" when the meeting ended, you're doing the world a favor by not allowing the food to go to waste.

Golf Slackers –

I've noticed on many occasions that slackers who golf do a variety of things to improve their score. One way, which is probably the best, is to be the scorekeeper. Even if those in your group ask what you got after each hole, they will never remember your score by the time the round is over. So cheat on your score, and cheat often.

Improving Your Lie –

Whenever your ball is in a position that is "unfavorable" why not "press" down on the ground directly behind the ball so your club head can make better contact. If you're just out of bounds, check and see that no one is looking, and slightly kick it back in bounds. You don't want to have to "drop" any more than necessary.

Then there is hitting your ball out of play (woods for instance) or in a lake. Either way, if it's unrecoverable its penalty enough to lose a ball, why have to count dropping one? Hit one, goes in lake, drop one, hit it and count it as two strokes, not three.

Now I did see my friend Dan the other day teeing it up in a bunker. I was so proud of him. This is an excellent way to get out of trouble. If no one sees you, they will think you have great skills at getting out of the sand so easily.

The latest way to improve your score is called a "Gore." Like our past VP, if you don't like your lie, or score, just holler "Gore" and improve your lie and score until you get what you want. Oh right, Gore was recounting votes in districts that he had already won heavily, hoping that the count would change with each new recount. You could always say you were in Denver recently and the high altitude affected your play.

Slacking on Vacation –

You might think that slacking on vacation is what vacation is all about, but there is a better way to vacation and spend very little money at the same time. It's called living off your relatives or friends? Always try to vacation with relatives that live in a good vacation state, perhaps Florida, California, Hawaii, or even Colorado.

When you vacation at a relative's house, you can use their accommodations- housing (big expense), water, food, car, etc. It's also very good not to have a long distance calling card or your own cell phone, that way you can use your relative's phone and put long distance charges on their bill. Better yet, an "Obamaphone" provided by the government would work too.

Never offer to pay for anything. If your relatives suggest you do, tell them you'll have to send them a check after they tally up all that you owe them. Then when they tell you the amount, you can say your letter got lost in the mail. Always use the old phrase "The check's in the Mail." You'll be able to put them off for months and sooner or later they will just give up trying.

Card Key Access –

If you have a card key/fob to enter the various buildings where you work, leave it at home every so often. That way you can have the excuse to go back home to get it. Has it ever stopped working? If it has, don't assume that this means you have to find an alternate way to enter the building? Some buildings are just too far to walk to. Maybe you should just go home and try again tomorrow?

Wives and Excuses –

Bub got a call from his wife the other day. The battery had died in her car. He left work at 11 am. We never saw him again until the next day. Apparently she couldn't handle things on her own. It took him all afternoon to replace the battery. Now that's slick slacking.

The Slacker's Work Schedule –

Starting Time	8:05 a.m.
Smoke Break	8:10 a.m. – 8:20 a.m.
Morning Coffee Break	9:00 – 11:30 a.m.
Lunch Hour	11:30 a.m. – 1:30 p.m.
Smoke Break	1:40 p.m. – 1:50 p.m.
Afternoon Coffee Break	2:00 – 4:30 p.m.
Quitting Time	4:45 p.m.

8 AM on a workday, it must be "Tennis time for Bub."

IEP –

If you ever have been in school, you know exams and labs are not always given at the same time. Some students will attend a lab on Tuesday, while the remaining students will attend on Thursday. If you're a smart slacker, you will form an IEP - Information Exchange Program. For instance, if a co-slacker is going to be taking a test before you, then perhaps they can "direct" you to what will be on the test, and thus what to study. I'm not advocating cheating here. I am advocating a shortcut. Why study more than you need to. That's not the Slacker way.

If a co-slacker has been through one of your chemistry classes and still has his old lab workbook, then why not see if there are any similarities, and thus reduce the amount of time you have to spend in lab; Work Smarter not Harder. Bub always told me to "Work Harder, not Smarter."

Marrying Up –

If you are inclined to marry someone you really don't love, then perhaps you might consider marrying an older man or woman. What better way to move up the economic ladder, and quickly! Does this sound familiar to you? I can think of a well know U.S. Senator with a yacht and millions to go along with it.

If they are widowed, make sure you don't sign any pre-nuptial agreement that prevents you from latching on to their various worldly goods. Your new spouse's kids will not like it very well if you weasel in on their expected inheritance. Pre-nuptials will work only if they are slanted your way. That way when your spouse does pass away, you will be home free.

Get the home, car, vacation home, and retirement plans in your name. Remove the children's names from as many valuables as possible. Leave no trace. If needed, talk him or her into leaving only a small pittance to their kids. That way you can say see, he didn't forget you.

If you have your own kids, see what you can do to add their names to the various holdings, stocks, bonds, boats, businesses, etc. If all works out as planned, you should be rolling in the dough within 5 to 10 years.

If your new spouse is in ill health, see if you can have his kids buy some LTC (long term care insurance) so the holdings aren't eaten alive by hospitals and nursing homes.

Always present yourself as acting in the best interest of your spouse. Never lose your temper, and if things start to get rough with your new relatives, act as if you're a victim in all this, and that you were only carrying out your late spouse's wishes.

Slacking at Home –

Now, I really don't slack much at home. I do relax, but remember, the work I do at home has a direct relationship on the quality of my personal life.

The Cat and the Litter Box –

Slacking at home is great, especially if you have kids. For instance, if you really don't like to empty the litter box, then come up with a chore list for the kids, not only will they now have to empty the litter box, in order to get their allowance, but you can assign other chores as well.

Procrastination Pays –

My slacker wife pulled a slick move the other day. She had noticed that the litter box needed to be emptied and she knew that I would be coming into the bathroom to get ready for work in a few minutes. She got in the shower as quickly as possible; knowing that once I noticed the smell from the litter box, I would feel compelled to clean it. Even if I am a slacker, I can't stand the smell of a dirty litter box. The one mistake she made was admitting to her little scheme. She's pretty honest.

A Man, His Castle, and the Lazy Boy –

Sometimes I'm sitting in my Lazy Boy, what a great name for a recliner, watching a Pacer's game or a NASCAR event, and I have run out of Coke and popcorn, and really don't want to get up to get some more. If you wait long enough, your wife or kids will be walking through and you can say, "hey, while you're up, would you please refill this for me?" It works every time.

Great Slacker Quotations –
- "May the best slacker win."
- "Nothing is certain but slackers and taxes."
- "There's a slacker born every minute."
- "No one ever got rich being a slacker." Wait, is that right?
- "No slacker ever built up a sweat by not working."
- "If you're not a slacker by age twenty, something is wrong with you, and if you're not a slacker by age forty, something is definitely wrong with you."
- "Change for the sake of change is not progress but stupidity."

- "There are managers that can't separate the important from the unimportant, and neither can slackers."
- "To err is Human, to be a human slacker, divine."
- "Working Would be Great…(Thoughts on Business, Life, and Slackers)"

There are many others. Add your own:

_____

_____

_____

_____

_____

Chapter 6: Closing

Slackers where I worked always denied their heritage, or what they had become. None really wanted to be thought of as a slacker, they just wanted the perks that came with it. Does anyone really want to be called a "Loser?" It's the same way when being dubbed a slacker.

I was talking with a co-worker one day, and discussing the different problems (I'm sorry they're called "opportunities" now) with our firm and related many of them to those managers running the show. We felt that perhaps they had some sort of disease, whether it was genetic, bacterial, or viral, we didn't know. Either way, I was sure I wouldn't test positive for whatever it was. He stated that I had worked there too long to not have been exposed. He ensured me that I would indeed test, Slacker Positive.

Slackers, embrace your heritage. Never deny what so many people have worked to perfect for so long. "Slackerism" is the new wave. Come out of the bathroom stall and declare your heritage, your right! Perhaps we can become a protected minority. Then again, it's probably too late, we're probably already the majority.

So in closing, may the manager you work for now and in the future have an IQ slightly higher than your average slacker and the disposition of a Sloth. If you're ever down because your boss or his boss has been riding your case as of late, then remember to look in the mirror and say this phrase first thing every morning (I think it's from the movie Johnny Dangerously) stand up straight, and with a big smile say "I'm smart, I'm beautiful, everybody loves me!" Good Slacking.

Acknowledgments:

My wife Tracy, without her patience this project wouldn't have been possible.

My daughter Jennifer, thank you so much for your support; helping me set up my web site, and for the great front cover you designed. If you would like to see more of her work, go to:
http://jennifernicholewells.com

Nelson Angel Gomez, Jr., my good friend and illustrator. The book wouldn't have been half as good without your drawings, thanks.

Terry Beaty, my good friend and encourager. Thanks for the ideas.

Ken Hudson, good friend, critiquer, and idea developer. Ken, your insight and help was greatly appreciated.

My older and wiser friend Dan, your critiquing and ideas helped make this book better. No Brown toothbrushes, okay?

My brother-in-law, Monte and his wife Jean, thank you for your encouragement.

Michael Schepps - You are such a good friend. Thank you for your support.

Franca Higginbotham – Thank you very much for the encouragement; you don't know how much it was appreciated.

About the Author:

Gary currently resides in Florida.
He is attempting to become a well-known author with the hope of never having to report to a manager like Bub ever again.
Gary has a B.S in Medical Technology and an MBA.
Gary can be contacted via his web site at:
garywwells.com
You can add your own stories and start a discussion. Keep it clean.

My Testimonials:

I read Gary's book and was astounded at his knowledge and depth about what really goes on in the corporate world. You won't find another book that tells you the "way it is."

The Slacker Tribune

Gary's book is funny, witty, cutting, and educational. His insight of the on-goings and failures of American corporations should ring a bell with all that read this. For those who want to be a slacker, or want to improve their skills, his chapter on "Slacker Fun Stuff" tops all else.

Slacker Henry Devine, President
Slacker Laboratories and HMO Services

Buy this book! Read this book! Buy it for all those lousy managers you have worked for.
This is a must read book for those who have been abused by their own managers. You will laugh and be angry all at the same time.

The Slacker Herald-Tribune

Slackers beware your secrets are out. Managers, your story has been captured and told!

Slacker News and Report

If this book isn't a best seller by the eighth week on the market, then America and the world need to take a good hard look at itself. This is good stuff!

John Johnson, CEO, CFO,
United Slacker's of America